MW01091987

GAME OF MY LIFE

SOUTH CAROLINA

GAMECOCKS

GAME OF MY LIFE

SOUTH CAROLINA

GAMECOCKS

MEMORABLE STORIES OF GAMECOCK FOOTBALL

RICK SCOPPE AND
CHARLIE BENNETT

SPORTS
PUBLISHING

Copyright © 2007, 2013 by Rick Scoppe and Charlie Bennett

Sports Publishing books may be purchased in bulk at special discounts for sales promotion, corporate gifts, fund-raising, or educational purposes. Special editions can also be created to specifications. For details, contact the Special Sales Department, Sports Publishing, 307 West 36th Street, 11th Floor, New York, NY 10018 or sportspubbooks@skyhorsepublishing.com.

Sports Publishing® is a registered trademark of Skyhorse Publishing, Inc.®, a Delaware corporation.

Visit our website at www.sportspubbooks.com.

10 9 8 7 6 5 4 3 2 1

Library of Congress Cataloging-in-Publication Data is available on file.

ISBN: 978-1-61321-333-9

Printed in the United States of America

CONTENTS

A WORD FROM THE HEAD BALL COACH

There have been a lot of outstanding football players at the University of South Carolina over the years. In this book, a number of them share their stories about the most memorable game they ever played for the Gamecocks. Hopefully, one of these days books will be written that go beyond individual players and individual games and chronicle great seasons. Here at South Carolina we're certainly working on putting together some of those seasons.

—Steve Spurrier

INTRODUCTION

It was in the spring of 2005 when a publisher approached Rick about doing a book about University of South Carolina football that focused on former players telling the stories of their most memorable games as a Gamecock.

Rick liked the idea, but decided it was more work than he wanted to take on alone, given he was also the USC beat writer for *The Greenville News*. So he enlisted me to help with the project. Over the months that followed, we interviewed some of the best football players in Gamecock history, and others who were not necessarily the best in team history, but rose to the occasion when called on.

What they all had in common was an interesting story to tell, and we felt the stories that followed were fascinating—like that of the late Dominic Fusci, whose career was interrupted by the outbreak of WWII, and resumed after he served in the Pacific on a PT boat tender.

Dom turned down a pro offer from the Washington Redskins to return to school at South Carolina, because as he put it, "I couldn't afford the pay cut."

Fortunately for the Gamecocks, the statute of limitations has long since run out on NCAA violations from the 1940s.

Another favorite includes the story of running back Ryan Brewer, a former Mr. Football in the state of Ohio, who would be spurned in recruiting by Ohio State only to eventually lead the Gamecocks to victory over the Buckeyes in the Outback Bowl.

There's also the story of Erik Kimrey, whose big game consisted of one play—coming in for an injured quarterback on fourth down and throwing for a game-winning touchdown.

Now with the addition of bonus material, this book is ready to receive a second chance.

We hope you enjoy it.

—Charlie Bennett

Authors' Note:

We have written new chapters on Alshon Jeffery and Marcus Lattimore for the re-release of this book. Nevertheless, we have preserved the rest of the text, as it was originally published in 2007. We would like to note that since the initial publication, Dominic Fusci (Chapter 23) has passed away.

Chapter 1

GEORGE ROGERS

THE YOUNG LIFE OF GEORGE ROGERS

Even at a young age, George Rogers was a gifted athlete, but football was a learning process. And the future Heisman Trophy winner admits he had a lot to learn when he first stepped on a football field as a youngster in Atlanta, Georgia, in the late 1960s.

"We used to play what we called, 'Throw it up,'" Rogers remembers. You just throw the ball up, somebody gets it, and then you have to tackle him. You just throw the ball all around.

"That's all I knew. I was about eight or nine when I went out for football. My first time out there, the quarterback said, 'Down, set, hut,' and threw me the football. I saw all those guys coming at me and threw it right back to him. Of course, I got hit, and knocked around. So they had to teach me how to play."

Rogers says the other players teased him and called him "butterfingers." As he began to learn more about the rules of the game, it was a label he was determined to shed.

"It came time for a game, and I had to walk three miles to get there," Rogers said. "I was going to show everybody that I knew what to do.

"We were playing this team called Avondale, and they were good. When I got to the game, the coach wasn't going to play me because he hadn't been there to see that they had taught me how to play. I had to do something to get in this game, so I started crying. I'm standing on the sideline and I'm hollering, 'I want to play, I want to play.' A lady in the stands said, 'Why is that little boy crying?' One of my friends said, 'He's crying because the coach won't let him play. He doesn't know how to play.' I said, 'I do know how to play, I do know how to play.' The lady said, 'Why don't they put him in the game? They're losing anyway.'"

Finally, the coach relented and put Rogers in the game.

"They pitched the ball right to me and I know he was expecting me to get killed again because that's all he had ever seen," he said. "They pitched the ball right to me and I was gone. I went down that sideline. I ran until there was no more grass left. My teammates came running down, I started dodging them, too. From then on, I was the man."

But times were hard on the home front. Rogers' father was in prison, and his mother was trying to raise five children by herself. He remembers a time when he almost didn't get to play youth league football because he didn't have $2 for insurance.

He also remembers one year when the youth league team was going to draw names at Christmas.

"I didn't have anything to give anybody," Rogers said. "I took my thigh pads and wrapped them up in aluminum foil as a gift. The guy who pulled my name bought me a model car that you put together."

Rogers played football up until his eighth grade year; a broken ankle suffered in a bicycle accident kept him out the next two years.

Before his 10th grade year, Rogers went to live with his aunt in nearby Duluth, Georgia. It proved to be a big turning point for him.

"She let me come live with her and she laid down the rules," he said. "I had to go to Sunday school and church. I had to do dishes. I was like, 'I'll do anything.' So I got to Duluth High School and I was anxious. I knew I could play, but I was anxious to see if I still had it."

George Rogers. *Photo provided by Collegiate Images/South Carolina*

Rogers did, but it was time for another football lesson. This one came courtesy of Duluth coach Cecil Morris.

"Getting the ball, I was running up in there tip-toeing and they would tackle me," Rogers said. "Before I could get up, Coach Morris had grabbed me. He lifted me up off the ground and started shaking me and started yelling at me, saying, 'What do you think you're doing? Run the damn ball.' What that did, that made me mad and I started running over everything in sight. He said, 'Now that's how you run the ball.' I finally scored a touchdown against North Gwinnett, and from then on I was scoring touchdowns."

By Rogers' senior year, he had attracted the attention of every major college coach in the South. He chose South Carolina mainly because coach Jim Carlen promised him the opportunity of immediate playing time.

THE SETTING

Carlen proved true to his word about immediate playing time for Rogers.

Playing primarily at fullback, Rogers rushed for a South Carolina freshman-record 623 yards on the Gamecocks' 5-7 football team in 1977.

Rogers settled in at fullback, with teammate Johnnie Wright showing promise as the Gamecocks tailback.

As a sophomore, Rogers rushed for 1,006 yards and six touchdowns, but changes were in store for the South Carolina offense.

"My junior year, me and Spencer Clark and Johnnie Wright were the running backs," Rogers said. "Spencer was a senior and me and Johnnie were juniors.

"Coach Carlen came to me in the spring and said, 'I'm putting you at tailback.' I was like, 'I'll play fullback. I don't care as long as I get the ball.' He was like, 'George, you're faster than he is and we need some speed.' Johnnie didn't want to play fullback, so we switched it back."

Then fate intervened. Wright went down with a knee injury, and Rogers moved back to tailback.

Rogers rushed for 1,681 yards his junior season, second in the nation behind Southern California's Charles White, who would go on to win the Heisman Trophy. Rogers didn't even make the top five in the Heisman balloting, finishing seventh.

But his junior season made people sit up and take notice, and the Gamecocks entered the 1980 season with the nation's leading returning rusher and a veteran offensive line.

What Rogers needed to solidify his status as a Heisman candidate was a big-time performance on a national stage. South Carolina's schedule in 1980 set up nicely for that, with back-to-back games in September on the road against Southern California and Michigan.

THE GAME OF MY LIFE
BY GEORGE ROGERS

My senior year, I was up for the Heisman Trophy, but I was looking at it as more of a team thing than an individual thing. I say that because our offensive linemen worked as hard as I worked and they wanted it as much as I did. We were up for the Heisman.

We whipped up on Pacific (37-0) and Wichita State (73-0) and then we had to go to Southern Cal and Michigan. I had a pretty good game against Southern Cal (141 yards rushing) and I think that helped, but we lost 23-17.

Now on the Michigan game, I think we were overexcited because it was the big boys playing the little boys in the Big House, and we of course were the little boys.

At Michigan they've got these two sides where you come out onto the field. They'll let you come out, but then they'll come out and just run right through the middle of you. After they did that, Coach Carlen told us, "If ya'll go out and whip Michigan, I'll go whip [Michigan coach] Bo Schembechler." That got us fired up. Let me tell you, it was on. When we got on that field, we went at them with all we had. We let them know they were in a game.

I had a good game, but that was because of the offensive line. They weren't very big, but one thing we knew how to do, we knew how to run the ball. You knew we were going to run the ball and you couldn't stop it. I know I went over 100 yards and scored a touchdown and we ended up winning the game 17-14. Michigan would go on to win the Rose Bowl, and we would go on to lose the Gator Bowl. But I think that game right there solidified that South Carolina was on the map, and maybe made people start thinking that maybe we did deserve to be considered for the Heisman.

You know what, though? After we beat Michigan, Coach Carlen didn't do what he said he was going to do. He didn't whip Bo Schembechler.

THE AFTERMATH

South Carolina may have come out of the locker room fired up to play Michigan, but it was the Wolverines who set the tone in the first half in front of a crowd of 104,213 in the "Big House."

The Gamecocks scored on a 26-yard field goal for a 3-0 lead, but Michigan came back to take a 14-3 lead at the half on two second-quarter touchdown passes from John Wangler to Anthony Carter.

Michigan opened the second half by driving to the South Carolina 8-yard line, but fullback Jerald Ingram fumbled in the end zone, with the Gamecocks' Walt Kater recovering for a touchback.

South drove it the other way, and 14 plays later, Rogers scored on a 2-yard run to cut the Wolverines' lead to 14-10 with 1:21 remaining in the third quarter.

Then in the fourth quarter, the Gamecocks got a break courtesy of an uncharacteristic gamble by the usually conservative Schembechler.

With the Wolverines facing fourth and inches from their own 30, Schembechler elected to go for it, but fullback Stan Edwards was stopped for a yard loss and the Gamecocks took over at the Michigan 29.

South Carolina drove for the go-ahead touchdown, a 1-yard run by Johnny Wright.

Michigan almost pulled it out, driving to the Gamecock 3-yard line, but South Carolina cornerback Chuck Finney batted down a fourth-down pass in the end zone on the final play of the game.

Rogers finished with 142 yards rushing, further cementing his credentials for the Heisman Trophy.

Looking back, Rogers' accomplishments as a running back at the University of South Carolina are staggering.

He finished his career at South Carolina with a school-record 5,024 rushing yards, including a single-season record 1,894 during his Heisman Trophy-winning senior year.

Rogers rushed for 100 or more yards 27 times, including 22 consecutive games.

He was the first player chosen in the 1981 NFL draft and earned NFL Rookie of the Year honors with the New Orleans Saints.

Between seasons of his pro career, Rogers came back to school at South Carolina to continue work on his college degree.

"It took a while, but I finally graduated," Rogers said. "I'm proud of that."

After eight years in the NFL, Rogers retired from professional football and came back to the Columbia area, where he has lived ever since.

He dabbles in private business ventures, works in South Carolina's Office of Student Affairs, and also helps oversee the George Rogers Foundation, a non-profit organization that funds scholarships for needy students at in-state schools.

He remains one of the University of South Carolina's best ambassadors.

And nearly every year, he returns to New York for the Downtown Athletic Club's annual presentation of the Heisman Trophy.

"I don't make it every year," Rogers said, "but I can tell you one thing. When I was having troubles, the Downtown Athletic Club was there for me. I was going through some bad times, and the Downtown Athletic Club said, 'You get back here.' It's a big fraternity and I really feel like they were one of the few who were on my side. And also the University of South Carolina. I owe the school a lot."

Chapter 2

DAN REEVES

THE YOUNG LIFE OF DAN REEVES

For someone who would go on to play or coach in an NFL-record nine Super Bowls, Dan Reeves came from humble but not unusual beginnings for a youngster in the deep south in the 1940s and 1950s. He was raised on a farm about six miles outside of Americus, in rural Georgia.

With that upbringing came a certain attitude that cropped up after Reeves had committed to the Gamecocks. Reeves wasn't heavily recruited. In fact, South Carolina was the only major school interested in Reeves, who didn't have to think long about accepting the offer.

"I couldn't sign that thing fast enough," Reeves said. "I wanted to sign that thing before they changed [their] mind."

A few small schools were interested in Reeves as a basketball player—he helped lead Americus High School to the state championship as a senior. A star two-sport athlete, Reeves was selected to the state's all-star team in both football and basketball. Reeves wound up playing in the football game. After not playing in the first half, Reeves led his team to a comeback victory and was named the game's most valuable player.

"Then we had a bunch of schools that came after me," Reeves said.

Marvin Bass, who was in his first year as South Carolina's head coach, got wind of the sudden upsurge in interest in Reeves and made his first trek to Americus to visit with Reeves, who had signed with South Carolina having never met Bass.

Bass and a couple assistants ate lunch with Reeves and his father when Bass got to the point of his visit.

"I'll never forget it," Reeves said. "He said, 'You know, son, I can't promise you're going to start at South Carolina,' and of course all these other schools had promised me that already."

But, Reeves recalled Bass saying, "We took a chance on you when nobody else wanted you, so we need to have your answer because we've got to make plans if you aren't coming as to what we're going to do."

"Well, that was right down my daddy's line," Reeves said. "My daddy loved that. So he said, 'Son, where you going to school?'"

What could Reeves say?

He remembered answering, "Daddy, it sounds like South Carolina's great. He said, 'I agree with you. Let's go to South Carolina.' So I told Coach Bass I was going to South Carolina."

THE SETTING

When Reeves arrived in Columbia, freshmen were not eligible. So he played on the freshman team and did something he had never done before; he watched a football game from the press box, where he saw senior quarterback Jim Costen run Bass' offense, which was more wide open than former coach Warren Giese's ground-oriented attack.

"[Observing from the press box] really helped me to learn a lot in what I would do, what I was looking for, what a quarterback reads and those kind of things," he said. "I had never been in the press box. It was a great way to learn the game."

So Reeves watched and learned—and was glad for the experience. On the practice field, along with learning the offense, Reeves figured out what his backfield mates—all of whom were from the North—were saying.

"I was the only southerner in the backfield, so they couldn't understand me, and I couldn't understand them for about the first two weeks," he said. "We had to get each other's drawl down before we could learn what the other one was talking about."

After his freshman year, Reeves spent the summer back in Americus working in his father's construction business. Back then, players didn't hang around campus to go to summer school and work out in preparation for the coming season.

Reeves returned to campus and earned the starting job, and on September 22, 1962, 18-year-old Reeves was the youngest starting quarterback in the nation when he led the Gamecocks against Northwestern in Evanston, Illinois.

South Carolina lost 37-20, although on Reeves' first college play, the Gamecocks scored on running left on a sweep—led by Reeves.

"The quarterback back then used to lead for the blocking," he said.

It would be a tough year for Reeves and the Gamecocks, who would go on to lose three games by five points or less and also tie Georgia to finish 4-5-1, losing to archrival Clemson 20-17 in the regular-season finale on November 24.

There were some heartbreaking moments. Against Georgia on October 6, South Carolina was leading 7-0 when Reeves, playing safety, went up to try to intercept a pass when a teammate crashed into him. Both players fell to the ground while Georgia receiver Michael Babb grabbed Larry Rakestraw's pass and turned it into a 68-yard touchdown with 1:26 left in the game.

In a 19-14 loss to North Carolina in Chapel Hill, Reeves hit Sammy Anderson at the goal line in the final seconds.

"I think he scores," Reeves said. "He had chalk all over his jersey. But they spotted the ball on the 1-inch line and we couldn't line up to run another play before the clock expired."

Along with the heartbreaking losses, there was the bizarre—and nothing was as bizarre as what happened on a kickoff against Duke in a 21-8 loss to the Blue Devils in Durham, North Carolina, on September 29.

Future NFL star linebacker Mike Curtis kicked off for Duke, and the Gamecocks were called for "a penalty that I don't think had ever been called in college football," Reeves said.

Not only was South Carolina whistled for holding, but the officials also gave the ball to Duke—right where the Gamecocks had returned the kickoff. "I went in at quarterback to run the first play," Reeves said, still incredulous all these years later, "and the official said it's Duke ball first-and-10."

After a 13-11 loss at Maryland the next week, the Gamecocks won their next three, beating Virginia 40-6, North Carolina State 17-6, and Detroit 26-13 in the Motor City with temperatures in the teens—the last college game Detroit ever played.

"Really and truly, I thought that was as cold as it gets," Reeves said, "until I was in Green Bay for the Ice Bowl."

The win at Detroit evened South Carolina's record at 4-4-1 as they headed to Death Valley to take on Clemson.

THE GAME OF MY LIFE
BY DAN REEVES

I came from Georgia. I knew about Georgia-Georgia Tech and what a big rivalry that was. But I remember being in the press box my freshman year when a South Carolina fraternity came out dressed up like the Clemson team. They went out on the field and the Clemson student body went crazy; they thought it was their football team. That's when they started acting like they were milking cows and there was the biggest fight you've ever seen. That's when I went, "Wow, this is a big-time rivalry."

I was big-time nervous. I've always felt that if you weren't nervous for a game, you weren't ready. So I was nervous. I knew what was on the line. We had a chance to have a winning season. We had a chance to beat our in-state rival. We had lost some close games. We could have been a much better football team than our record showed, and here was a chance for us to end up with a winning record. So it was a big, big football game.

All I saw was orange coming out, everywhere. That moment was what college football was all about—being in a big atmosphere like that, in a big game, in a big rivalry. That was the biggest game I'd ever played in my life.

We had them down at halftime. I actually threw a pass for a touchdown that would have put us up 21-7, but it was called back because they said we had an ineligible receiver down field. I remember looking at the film, and that wasn't the case. I scrambled around but we didn't have anybody down field. I just think the official got lost with where the line of scrimmage was because it was one of those plays where the quarterback scrambles.

When they went ahead 20-17, Billy Gambrell made a tremendous kickoff return and gave us an opportunity. We were down in field goal range but went for the win instead of going for the tie. You didn't have overtime back then. If we won the game, we might have had the chance to go to a bowl. If we tied it, we wouldn't.

Of course, being a quarterback and having four shots at the end zone and not getting it there was disappointing. Coach Bass certainly made the decision to go for the win. There wasn't any hesitation on my part. We wanted to win the game.

It was just a tough loss for us. We had a lot of tough losses that year. We had a lot of close games, games that we could very easily have won. We could have easily had three more wins, therefore winning seven or eight football games. That would have been an unbelievable year.

THE AFTERMATH

South Carolina would win only four games in Reeves' final two seasons. The Gamecocks were 1-8-1 in 1963. Five of the losses were by nine points or less, including a season-ending 24-20 loss to

Clemson—a game that was postponed from November 23 to November 28 because of the assassination of President John F. Kennedy.

In 1964, South Carolina started 0-1-2, with ties against Duke and Georgia, but then lost four straight before ending the year with three victories, including a 7-3 win at Clemson behind reserve quarterback Jim Rogers, who came on for Reeves after he hurt his ankle.

"It was really tough for me physically because I ended up hurting my knee in the spring practice between my sophomore and junior year," Reeves said. "Having surgery on my knee, I ended up with both knees banged up for most of my junior year.

"Then my senior year, I thought we were going to have a really good team. It ended up being disappointing."

Off the football field, Reeves received an offer to join the basketball team from coach Frank McGuire, who had just been hired.

"I thought that was kind of neat," Reeves said. That is, until he found out what his role would be: "He said, 'I want you to be my hatchet man.' Hatchet man? What do you mean?"

"He said, 'They've got great players on the other team—that Billy Cunningham at North Carolina. I'll put you in there, and I want you to foul him four or five times. You might get into a fight. They throw both of you out and we've got rid of a good player.'

"Those guys he was talking about were like 6-5, 6-6, same weight as I was, but a lot bigger. I said, 'Coach, I don't think I want to be a hatchet man.'"

With that decision and his football career over, Reeves wasn't sure what was going to happen. He knew he wasn't good enough to play quarterback in the NFL. He was more of a running quarterback who, in his words, "could throw halfway decent."

"But," he added, "I didn't consider myself a passer."

Reeves wasn't drafted, but the reigning AFL champion San Diego Chargers were interested in him at safety. The Dallas Cowboys also called. They told Reeves they'd take a look at him at several positions, including safety but also running back and wide receiver.

"That attracted me because I felt that if I didn't make it there, maybe I'd get a shot in the new league. And also they promised they would try me at a lot of different positions," Reeves said.

So Dallas it was. Reeves spent eight years playing for coach Tom Landry and the Cowboys, playing in exactly 100 games. In 1966 he rushed for a career-high 757 yards and eight touchdowns while also catching 41 passes for 557 yards and eight touchdowns.

But Reeves' second NFL season was memorable mainly for one game—the 1967 championship battle against the Packers in Green Bay in the Ice Bowl on New Year's Eve. Green Bay won 21-17 on Bart Starr's quarterback sneak with 13 seconds left.

"I tell you what, for an ol' southern boy, I thought as soon as it got to freezing it couldn't get any worse," Reeves said. "I did not realize that. It was 15 degrees on Saturday when we worked out, and it was nice. We worked up a sweat, the sun was shining.

"The next day, it was 13 below and the wind was blowing and there was no sun. I did not realize [a change like] that was like going from 70 degrees to 102 degrees. You could feel every degree of it."

In 1967, Reeves rushed for 603 yards and also caught 39 passes for 490 yards. But a year later, after tearing up his knee, Reeves knew his playing days would soon come to an end. In 1969, Reeves got beat out by Calvin Hill, who went on to be the NFL's Rookie of the Year.

"After the '69 season, Coach Landry called me in and asked me if I'd be interested in being a player-coach," Reeves said. "I had never thought about coaching. I thought, 'Well this will be a good idea. I'd never heard of them cutting a coach. They get fired, but they don't get cut.'

"So I thought I'd stay around for a while. I ended up being a player-coach in '70 and '71, and we went to the Super Bowl those seasons. So I thought this was the greatest profession in the world."

In 1973, Reeves left coaching for the real estate business. But the coaching bug had bitten. So he returned to the NFL as an assistant, and in 1981, he was named the head coach for the Denver Broncos, leading them to three Super Bowls in 12 years.

In 1993, Reeves took over the struggling New York Giants and promptly led them to an 11-5 record and the playoffs—and earning coach of the year honors. But he was fired after the 1996 season. He wasn't out of work for long, however, accepting the head-coaching job with the Atlanta Falcons.

Reeves took a team that was 3-13 and led it to a 14-2 record and the Super Bowl, where the Falcons lost to the Broncos 34-19. But Reeves was fired near the end of the 2003 season, ending an NFL career in which he made it to the Super Bowl nine times, including an 0-4 record as a head coach.

"Certainly that's not a record you like, not winning the Super Bowl. But as a head coach I got there four times. I got there as a player, a player-coach, and an assistant coach five times. We ended up winning two and ended up on the losing end seven times," he said.

"You hate to get there and lose it. There's nothing worse. You remember that. It's the last game of the season. Not many people can tell you who the losing teams are in the Super Bowl. I probably can tell you more losing teams than anybody because seven times I lost it."

Looking back on his career at South Carolina and the NFL, Reeves said it "just goes to show anything's possible."

"I don't think coming out of high school that I was necessarily that talented. But through hard work and a lot of things like that, you can accomplish a heck of a lot," he said. "I was at the right place at the right time, surrounded by a lot of good people. I was truly, truly blessed.

"When I look at it, sometimes I wonder, why me, Lord? To think that He picked [me] when there could have been a lot of other people to have the opportunity that I had, I just am truly thankful that the good Lord blessed me with the ability and opportunity to do the things that I've done."

Chapter 3

TODD ELLIS

THE YOUNG LIFE OF TODD ELLIS

Todd Ellis grew up in the middle of basketball–crazy North Carolina. As a young teenager standing 6-foot-2, Ellis dreamed of playing center for the Tar Heels and coach Dean Smith. But Ellis stopped growing, and as he got older it was clear his talents lay elsewhere, although he backed up Danny Manning, who went on to Kansas and later the NBA.

With six of the basketball team's players going on to sign Division I scholarships—not including Ellis, who had signed a football scholarship—Greensboro Page High School won the state basketball title. So dominant was Page that Ellis actually got to play more than one might expect.

"We were killing teams so much I probably averaged six or seven minutes a game, which is unbelievable when you're backing up Danny Manning," Ellis said. "I was a blue-collar guy. I was just a bruiser, a banger."

Page High School was so good that Haywood Jeffires, who went on to play football for North Carolina State and then in the NFL, beat out Manning as Page's Most Valuable Player that season, Ellis said.

Ellis was recruited by North Carolina—for football.

"One of my greatest memories of being recruited was going to Chapel Hill and sitting on the bench with them at the Blue-and-White game in the spring and then Dean taking me to his office and showing me all his video screens," Ellis said.

"I still have a hand-written letter from Dean Smith after that visit because I respected him so much."

Ellis also played shortstop and pitched in baseball growing up, and ran track as a senior to work on his agility and speed. But during Ellis' three years in football, Page High School lost only two games and captured two state titles.

Every school wanted Ellis, who was considered the nation's top quarterback prospect. His family gave coaches "a list of rules on how to recruit [him]," which included "a flow chart" of his priorities. Ellis didn't want to play for any northern schools, except possibly Notre Dame or Penn State.

"That was a long process. I didn't answer the phone in my house for two years," he recalled as he sat in his law office. "My mom and dad did. We had rules on when [recruiters] could call."

South Carolina coach Joe Morrison adhered to those rules, calling Ellis like clockwork every Friday at about 7:40 a.m., just before Ellis headed to the bus stop to go to school. They would talk for about six minutes and then Morrison would hang up.

"That was of course game day. He'd just talk to me about what they were doing that weekend. That's all he did," Ellis said. "I respected that so much because I knew he was going to call at that time. He didn't barrage me the rest of the week."

Morrison left that to assistant coach Jim Washburn.

"Jim would call me up and he wouldn't say anything, wouldn't say hello or nothing. He'd get me on the phone and he'd say, 'You just got to ... are you tough? Are you the guy that can handle the challenge? You want to step outside what everybody else is telling you what to do? Come to South Carolina and you can lead us,'" Ellis said. "Then he'd hang up. He wouldn't even listen to me."

Ultimately, it came down to South Carolina or Stanford, which was coached by Jack Elway. While on his official visit to Stanford,

Todd Ellis. *Photo provided by Collegiate Images/South Carolina*

Ellis was taken to the Super Bowl in Palo Alto, California, where he was joined by Elway's son, Denver Bronco quarterback John Elway.

"That was unbelievable," Ellis said.

But Stanford was just too far for Ellis and his family. With the Gamecocks preparing for the 1984 Gator Bowl, Coach Morrison flew to Greensboro from Jacksonville, Florida, a couple days before Christmas.

"It's like 10 o'clock and all of a sudden there's a knock on the front door. My brother goes to the front door—you can't see it from the den," Ellis said. "I hear this, 'Ho, ho, ho little boy, is your brother here?'

"All of a sudden he came through the den. It was Joe Morrison in a Santa Claus suit with a blown-up scholarship that had a ribbon around it that had my name on it. He gave me the scholarship, and we took a couple pictures.

"He took his beard off. My mom made him a plate of turkey. He drank two Michelob Lites and got back on the plane. I never really told that story until he passed away because I didn't want people to know that. But that was stepping outside the bounds for him to do that, the guy in black, the conservative guy."

No one, not even Ellis and his parents, could turn down Santa Claus.

THE SETTING

After being red-shirted in 1985, Ellis shattered NCAA freshman records in 1986, throwing for 3,020 yards and 20 touchdowns, throwing for 200 yards or more in 10 of 11 games while completing what was then a school-record 60.3 percent.

Only Heisman Trophy winner Vinny Testaverde threw for more touchdowns (26) than Ellis. But the Gamecocks finished 3-6-2, which included a season-ending tie with archrival Clemson.

In 1987 South Carolina finished 8-4 behind Ellis, who became the program's career record leader in passing yards, attempts, and completions while throwing for 3,206 yards.

The highlight was a 20-7 win over Clemson on November 21 on ESPN, in a rare game between the two rivals when both were nationally ranked—South Carolina twelfth, and the Tigers, eighth. It was Morrison versus Danny Ford, two veteran coaches who by Ellis' estimation were at the peak of their careers.

"It was electric in that place that night. I probably played one of my smarter games, where I just didn't force anything, didn't feel like I had to make every play," said Ellis, who believes his school-record 73 interceptions will never be broken. "I remember eating the ball a lot. I remember making safe throws."

But one throw that wasn't safe stands out all these years later. South Carolina was backed up near its own end zone with third-and-long. Ellis rolled out, threw back across the field to Ryan Bethea, giving the Gamecocks a 77-yard gain, moving them to the Clemson 6-yard line.

"I half slipped, caught my balance, and Michael Dean Perry was coming right at me," Ellis said. "I stepped and threw. It was a risky throw but we had to have the first down. That was a huge win late in the season against a rival on a national stage where I played one of my smarter games."

But after two years in the run-and-shoot attack, Morrison hired Al Groh as offensive coordinator. Groh, whom Ellis said had a "brilliant mind," installed more of a pro-set scheme.

Ellis was worried South Carolina didn't have the personnel to make the most of the change. His offensive line was inexperienced. Robert Brooks was yet to display the talents that would make him one of the NFL's best wide receivers. Still, the Gamecocks won their first six games en route to a second straight 8-4 record.

In the midst of that streak was a 23-10 win for the 14th-ranked Gamecocks over Georgia in front of 73,800 fans at Williams-Brice Stadium. That day, Ellis completed 28 passes to nine different receivers for 321 yards. Defensively, South Carolina held Georgia, which led the nation in rushing—at 355.3 yards a game—to 102 yards, with 73 of those yards coming on the Bulldogs' first and last possessions.

THE GAME OF MY LIFE
BY TODD ELLIS

Georgia was extremely good on defense. I remember us trying to come up with a plan. They were kind of an all-or-nothing defense at the time. They either blitzed completely or dropped back and rushed three. It was very important that we pick up the keys because we weren't a very good running team at that time. Al and I worked really hard at getting those keys down and there were a lot of checks he had given me at the line. So I remember there being—certainly that season and maybe as much as any time in my career—the necessity for my ability to change the play at the scrimmage.

It was a hot, miserable day. They came out and did everything just like we thought they would do. We just got lucky and Robert had the game of his life. It was unbelievable, the catches that he made. I remember starting to know their keys. So I felt totally in control at the line of scrimmage. Every time they'd sneak and make a move, I'd check off to one of the quick routes to him or to one of the other receivers and get rid of it on a hot. I could see they were getting frustrated as the game went on.

Robert had seven or eight catches, but the play I'll always remember in my career is when we had a penalty right at midfield or at about their 40-yard line, and it backed us up. I had called a play where Robert was to run a 'go' route if the other team got into a certain look, and they got into it. But then we had the penalty. So I told Al, "Run it again, run it again, call it again." And so he called it again.

We got up to the line of scrimmage and Ben Smith, who was a great corner for them and went on to play for the Philadelphia Eagles, was out there on top of Robert, to the wide side of the field. It was like third-and-nine or something like that. He jammed him and Robert went to the corner.

I lofted one down there to the outside and Robert did an unbelievable job of just leaning on him. He caught it one-handed, with the nose right down in the top of his hand as it dropped. He put his foot down in the corner of the end zone and fell out of bounds. The place just went crazy. It's still the most unbelievable catch I've ever seen.

I used to just run to the sideline after plays. You know, I'd seen a few touchdowns in my day. But I was so pumped that I just ran right down to him and hugged him in the end zone. That moment made a full two-page shot in *Sports Illustrated*. We went on to win the game. But really, after that play, it was over with.

It was just one of those games; it was on a big stage, and we felt really good, and then Robert made that catch. I still have that issue of *Sports Illustrated*. I can't tell you where 90 percent of my memorabilia is, but I've got that.

THE AFTERMATH

South Carolina would go on to lose four of its last six, including a 34-10 loss to Indiana in the Liberty Bowl. A few weeks later, Morrison died of a heart attack after playing racquetball at Williams-Brice Stadium. Sparky Woods, an up-and-coming coach from Appalachian State, replaced Morrison.

The Gamecocks were 5-1-1 when Ellis' career ended in a 20-10 loss to N.C. State on October 28, 1989, when he injured his knee. Ellis tried to roll with the hit, but to no avail. It was, he said "a very disappointing way" for his record-setting career to end.

Ellis was picked in the ninth round of the NFL draft by the Denver Broncos but was later cut. He played one year for Sacramento in the World League but decided it was time to get on with the rest of his life, opting to go to law school and ending his football career for good.

"You make decisions and you go forward with them," Ellis said. "Probably the biggest part of my career that I regret was that I tried to do too much. I think I had better teams around me. I'm not sure it would have ended up in wins and losses that much more but I would have been a better player for South Carolina and for myself.

"I forced things at times, certainly with the interceptions. I wasn't the guy that had to make every play."

But the good memories far outweigh the bad. There was the time Ellis was coming out of the dorm when an attractive young coed accosted him.

"She said, 'Aren't you Todd Ellis?' I said, 'Yeah,'" Ellis recalled. "She came up and gave me a big ol' kiss. I said, 'This job is great!'"

There was also the moment that still remains in his memory when Ellis spoke briefly with Clemson quarterback Rodney Williams at midfield at Death Valley before the Gamecocks and Tigers did battle.

"He said, 'You realize we're the most powerful people in South Carolina right now?'" Ellis said. "If you realize that kind of responsibility and how good you've got it, then I think you appreciate that a little bit more. It was an awesome ride."

Chapter 4

STEVE TANEYHILL

THE YOUNG LIFE OF STEVE TANEYHILL

Steve Taneyhill grew up a coach's son—his father was a highly successful girls' basketball coach—who never dreamed that one day he'd be following in the old man's footsteps. But he does concede that basketball was his first love, at least partly because his father coached the sport.

But then, he added, you couldn't play football competitively in Altoona, Pennsylvania, until the fourth grade. So what was a third-grader to do?

"We also had a full court in our backyard," Taneyhill said. "That kind of helps you play basketball."

Taneyhill was born into a family of competitors. Along with his father's coaching exploits, his mother was a national baton-twirling champ and his sister won a basketball scholarship to George Mason.

"Our dinner table was interesting," Taneyhill said. "It was very competitive because we all had things going on. My teams weren't always as good but I got more attention. It was never really football until I got older and into high school, and then I had two things to talk about whereas everyone else had just one."

From his earliest days, Taneyhill was competitive. After his first Little League team—which had never won a championship—finished 2-23, Taneyhill led it to titles in his last two years.

Taneyhill also was cocky. While in junior high, Taneyhill told his parents one night at the dinner table that he would lead the Altoona High School team to the state finals, a feat it had not accomplished in nearly three decades.

And he almost did—with some help from future NBA player Danny Fortson, who was two years behind Taneyhill. Altoona lost in the finals his junior and senior years, but Taneyhill scored more than 1,400 points to set the school career record.

For the longest time, it appeared basketball would be Taneyhill's ticket to college. But as a junior Taneyhill came on in football. After a 1-4 start, Altoona won its last six games as Taneyhill helped engineer last-minute drives in five of those games—the only winning season for Taneyhill at Altoona in football.

"More team success basically came with basketball," he said. "As for individual success, more accolades came in football."

So while he continued to play basketball, Taneyhill focused his attention on landing a football scholarship. Notre Dame asked him to come to South Bend, Indiana, on an unofficial visit when he was a junior.

"So things started happening that made my decision, 'All right, let's go play football,'" Taneyhill said.

The Taneyhill home was "pretty crazy" during recruiting. Taneyhill said he'd get 10 or 15 calls a day from coaches.

"It just felt like you didn't have any free time," he said. "I didn't spend much time at home. I had something like 80 offers. You try to get that down to go on a visit. It's tough."

Ultimately, Taneyhill made only two official visits, canceling trips to UCLA, Miami, and Florida State. He flew to Columbia, South Carolina, and watched Clemson whip South Carolina 41-21 on November 23, 1991. Then he returned home to watch his sister play for George Mason and then flew back out to Tuscaloosa, to visit Alabama.

Steve Taneyhill. *Photo provided by Collegiate Images/South Carolina*

Why South Carolina? He thought the Gamecocks looked like an up-and-coming team with a lot of talented young players, and he hit it off with assistant coach Rich Bisaccia.

And Columbia was 10 hours from home. Tuscaloosa was 19.

THE SETTING

The pony-tailed Taneyhill made news even before his first practice. Watching the 1992 spring game, Taneyhill predicted he would be starting before the season was over—and he was right, although many didn't like the attitude of this brash Yankee.

And showing that his comments were no slip of the tongue, Taneyhill reiterated his prediction again on South Carolina's team picture day in August.

In between, Taneyhill attended the second session of summer school and got to know his teammates, going out and throwing with the receivers two or three nights a week. Taneyhill doubted they were impressed.

"That isn't, and never really was, my strong suit, just going out there and throwing," he said. "They were probably thinking, 'Man, this guy isn't very good. He doesn't throw tight spirals. He doesn't know what he's doing.'"

Taneyhill went into the fall fifth on the depth chart, a position he didn't take seriously and doubted the coaches did, either.

"That's what was on paper. Did I really believe that? The answer is no. Did the coaches really believe that? I don't know, but I would say they probably didn't," he said. "But that's how it was listed."

Taneyhill, who was 0-4 with two interceptions in two brief appearances in the first four games, got his chance against Alabama. While the eventual national champion rolled over South Carolina 48-7 on October 3, Taneyhill completed 10 of 17 passes for 135 yards.

"I didn't start, but I played pretty well," he said, "and I finished the game, most importantly."

The Gamecocks had an open date the next week, and Taneyhill said he took all the reps with the starting unit at practice. Coach Sparky Woods had not yet told the team Taneyhill would start in two weeks against No. 15 Mississippi State.

But Bisaccia, on a flight to Pittsburgh on a recruiting trip, had told Taneyhill, who was on the same airplane headed home.

"I said, 'Well, then we're going to win,'" Taneyhill said. "When I got back to Altoona that weekend, I just told everybody, 'Hey, I'm starting and we're going to win.' That's how I really felt. It wasn't me just being cocky."

When Taneyhill returned to Columbia on Sunday night, he learned a players-only meeting had been called, where the players, some wanting Woods to resign, threatened to mutiny if some changes weren't made.

"At that point, I was a big recruit but I hadn't done anything. They just asked everybody, 'What are you going to do?' For me it was easy; I was 19 years old. I wasn't going to go against these guys that I was going to have to play with regardless of what happened." Taneyhill said. "It was a strange couple of days."

Ultimately, the players backed down, thanks mainly to the efforts of assistant coach Tommy West. "He was so well respected by the players," Taneyhill said. "He said, 'Okay, guys, we're going to figure this out but we've got a game Saturday. And we need to go practice today.' And so we did."

And as Taneyhill predicted, the Gamecocks won. South Carolina rolled up 505 yards in total offense—322 on the ground en route to a stunning 21-7 victory behind a freshman quarterback making his first college start.

This was not the same team that had been outscored 154 to 47 in its first five games.

"It was pretty unbelievable," Taneyhill said.

After a 21-17 win at Vanderbilt the next week, the Gamecocks shocked No. 16 Tennessee 24-23 on Halloween when linebacker Hank Campbell—Taneyhill's roommate—stopped James Stewart on a two-point conversion with 53 seconds left in the game.

After a 14-13 win over Louisiana Tech and a 14-9 loss to Florida in Gainesville, Taneyhill's first trip to Death Valley to face Clemson loomed. It was a game that will be remembered not primarily because the Gamecocks won 24-13, but because of Taneyhill's two home run swings and signing his name, figuratively speaking, to the tiger paw at midfield.

THE GAME OF MY LIFE
BY STEVE TANEYHILL

Every day before practice, they'd show us a video clip of us getting beat the year before, or a big play and the fans. And it built it up. I didn't know on Monday what that game was going to be like from a rivalry standpoint. I think the first time I realized it was maybe Friday when we actually got to Clemson.

We always went on the field the day before the game and kind of walked around and threw the football around. But there were a lot of media and people there when we got off the bus. I felt it right then and there; this was very different from all our other games that year.

When we got there Friday for our walk-through, it was me, Brandon Bennett, Rob DeBoer, Toby Cates, and Asim Penny, and we were all playing around near the 5-yard line. We were joking around, pretending to dive, falling down, seeing if we could reach the end zone from there.

I remember that being on the news that night. It showed us clowning around and having fun. I think the headline was, "Are the Carolina guys overconfident? They seem real loose." We were just doing what we normally did on Fridays, just having fun. All of a sudden, everything we did was big.

And my high school coach came to that game. I got to see him Friday night. Those type of things made it big from my standpoint, not so much the rivalry, but anytime your high school coach travels 10 hours to see you play, it's got to be important.

Coming out of the locker room, coach Sparky Woods held us up and said we weren't going out first. We were going to let them come down, and when they got impatient and came down the hill, we were going to steal their applause.

At the start, Clemson drove down and kicked a field goal. So when we got the ball, we were already down. I remember the first pass I threw. It was a little in route to Asim, maybe for 15 yards, and then we ran two plays and then on a big third down, I hit Toby down the sidelines for a big gain. We ended up getting the ball down to the five or the four and we got a penalty. I think Rob DeBoer got in an argument with one of their players and they gave us a 15-yard penalty; we ended up back on like the 20-yard line on third down.

I scrambled out and I threw one that only Asim could catch. Asim was about 6-5. He was a former basketball player. He caught it right on the pylon for the touchdown. Just how it happened— Clemson scoring first and then us turning around and coming back down and scoring and the way we did it—that gave everybody confidence.

I think the next important thing is I threw a pick towards the end of the first half and they returned it for a touchdown. So we were losing. I came to the sidelines and I was upset. It was a tipped interception, but it was still an interception returned for a touchdown. I was pretty down and a lot of the guys came up and said, "Hey, you've got to go out there and be the leader on the offense. You can't have your head down. We haven't seen you act like this all year. Come on."

We went out and drove it down and kicked a field goal to tie it at the half. So we went into halftime 10-10, but we felt good because we just did the two-minute drive and we got down there and Marty Simpson kicked a field goal and here we were, tied. And our defense had really only given up that one drive. I gave Clemson the other one.

To start the second half, we ran the ball. Brandon and Rob just running, running, running, and we got down to the 25 or so, and they called a little play action and Toby ran a corner route. That was my favorite pass play. It had been our first pass play at Mississippi State in my first start. To this day, as a coach, I call that play more than any other play. It's my favorite play.

I hit Toby in the corner of the end zone and he dove and caught it. That was a drive that really I didn't have anything to do with except for the last play. At that point, once we took the lead and because our defense had played so well, that was kind of the turning point.

We didn't do too much else. In the fourth quarter, we had another long drive to seal it. But Brandon did all the work. I think we actually did run it every single play on that drive except maybe one pass.

THE AFTERMATH

Throughout his remembrance of the game, Taneyhill didn't once mention his home run swings or signing the tiger paw. But when questioned, he reflected on what fans on both sides will likely never forget.

"The home run [swing] after Asim's touchdown, I did it. That was kind of already decided. That just didn't happen. Just the guys hanging out, I said, 'Let me get the opportunity to celebrate.'

"Then after I threw the second touchdown pass, Rob stopped me and pretended to throw one up to me. So I basically did the same thing twice, but one time I was by myself and one time Rob was there."

But that was nothing compared to the uproar caused by his unauthorized autograph.

"The signing of the paw was actually after Brandon Bennett made a long run down the sideline. I was just jogging down. He got knocked down. The refs were moving the ball and I was just headed that way," Taneyhill said.

"When I came across it—that was on the last drive—I felt like we were going to win anyway. I just knelt down and pretended to sign it. At that time, I thought nothing of it. I just thought it was funny. But obviously it turned into something way bigger than that because I still hear about it today.

"I don't even know that any of my teammates saw me do it because Brandon Bennett was going down the sideline. But it has turned out to be one of those things that still today, 14 years after the fact, people say they remember."

And to think Taneyhill still had three years left to play.

"How does it get any better?" he said. "It was unbelievable, I'll tell you."

After South Carolina finished 4-7 in 1993, the next season Taneyhill helped lead the Gamecocks under first-year coach Brad Scott to the first bowl victory in history, a 24-21 win over West Virginia in the Carquest Bowl.

It is a game that has grown in importance for Taneyhill with each passing year.

"That means something to me today," he said. "Here I am, going to be inducted into the Sports Hall of Fame at Carolina, and that's important and it's a great honor. But you look back and you say, 'I've got these records, but with coach Steve Spurrier there now, they really don't stand a chance.'

"But winning that first bowl game, you can't take that away from us. I'm just happy to be a part of it."

As a senior, Taneyhill put together an unforgettable individual season, which was highlighted by his school-record 473 yards passing—he completed 38 of 44 passes—in a 65-39 win at Mississippi State on October 14, 1995.

"That's the best game I've ever played in my entire life," he said.

His career over, Taneyhill took a stab at the NFL, but he was cut by the Jacksonville Jaguars. He played briefly in NFL Europe before retiring to become—of all things—a coach, first at Cambridge Academy in Greenwood, South Carolina, and now at Chesterfield High School.

"[Assistant] coach [John] Reaves and Coach Scott told me, 'You're going to be a football coach.' I said there's no way. I don't have the patience," Taneyhill said. "And here I am coaching high school football. I've told people it's the closest you can get to actually playing when your playing career is done.

"I hope one day to coach one more game inside the stadium. But the only way to do that would be in the state championship game. So I've got some things to achieve yet."

Chapter 5

RYAN
BREWER

THE YOUNG LIFE OF RYAN BREWER

Ryan Brewer was almost lost to football at an early age. Brewer's first love was soccer, and growing up in Troy, Ohio, it was a sport he remembers playing almost as soon as he could walk.

"I loved soccer and I was good at it," Brewer said. "I played all the time growing up. I was on a couple national teams."

However, Brewer began playing football in the fifth grade and quickly became adept at that sport as well. He started out as a running back, and led the local peewee league in touchdowns in his very first season. Still, Brewer maintains he was a much better soccer player, and he continued to play both sports up until his junior year in high school, when he was faced with a fateful decision.

"My regional [soccer] coach told me I had to choose between soccer and football if I expected to make the national team," Brewer recalls.

Brewer chose football.

"I loved soccer, but I guess by that time I loved football more," he said. "My mom—and even my dad, who is an avid football fan— wonder what would have happened if I had played soccer because that was my best sport. Oh yeah, I was a lot better in soccer."

Maybe so, but Brewer was no slouch in football.

In 1998, during his senior season in high school, Brewer rushed for an Ohio single-season record 2,864 yards, capping a career that saw him finish with 7,651 yards and 761 points scored. He was selected Ohio's Mr. Football after his senior year. *Ohio Prep Magazine* selected him as the Ohio High School Player of the 1990s.

Like almost everyone in Troy, Brewer was an Ohio State fan, but by the time he was wrapping up an all-star high school career, he already knew he wasn't destined to be a Buckeye.

"We lived an hour west of the Ohio State campus," Brewer said. "It's Ohio State country. That's all anyone talked about it. If you drive through there with Michigan plates, you get spit on. Ohio State kept leading me on, leading me on. I probably went to eight or nine Ohio State games in a two-year span. They kept saying, 'This is the day coach [John] Cooper is going to offer you a scholarship.' But my junior year, they didn't invite me to camp. It was clear they were no longer interested. It was disappointing."

Brewer was also a big Notre Dame fan. Although the Fighting Irish didn't offer a scholarship either, Brewer figured the next best thing might be playing for former Notre Dame coach Lou Holtz, who had just taken the head coaching job at South Carolina.

The way Holtz tells the story, Brewer called him up and committed before a scholarship offer was even made.

Brewer's version is slightly different. He says he had already talked with assistant coaches Skip Holtz and Dave DeGuglielmo, and had been offered a scholarship before he ever talked with Lou.

Either way, Brewer became a Gamecock.

"I was excited about playing for Lou Holtz," Brewer said. "The man is a legend."

THE SETTING

When Lou Holtz came out of retirement in 1999 to coach the South Carolina Gamecocks, he found the program in a shambles.

The Gamecocks were coming off a disastrous 1-10 season, and while former coach Brad Scott had left a sprinkling of promising

Ryan Brewer. *Photo provided by Collegiate Images/South Carolina*

talent behind, there wasn't nearly enough on hand to compete in the Southeastern Conference.

Holtz had two things to sell to prospective recruits—his reputation as a builder of programs, and immediate playing time.

In addition to Brewer, Ohio's Mr. Football, Holtz's initial signing class included running back Andrew Pinnock, Connecticut's Mr. Football, and running back Derek Watson, the state of South Carolina's Mr. Football.

"I remember one day at one of the early practices before our freshman year, Derek and I were out on the field catching punts," Brewer said. "Coach Holtz walked over and said, 'You guys better be ready because you're going to play and you're going to play a lot.'"

However, things at South Carolina were destined to get worse before they got better.

South Carolina went 0-11 in 1999, getting outscored 278-87 and ending the season with the nation's longest losing streak—21 games.

"The toughest thing was going to class and being around your peers," Brewer said. "I didn't even want to wear my Gamecock football stuff."

As promised, Watson and Brewer, along with Pinnock, got plenty of playing time, but took a pounding behind the Gamecocks' inexperienced offensive line.

Brewer didn't care about the pounding.

"When you're a freshman, you just want to play," he said. "Every game, we were in it. We may have been 0-11, but we were in it. We had fans coming up after games saying, 'Thank you.' I'm like, 'What for? We lost.' And they would say, 'Yeah, but you gave effort.' We knew something special was going to happen."

Entering the 2000 season riding a 21-game losing streak, the Gamecocks quickly became one of the big stories in college football, winning their first four games en route to a 7-4 record and an invitation to play in the Outback Bowl in Tampa, Florida.

The opponent? Ohio State.

The plot thickened when Derek Watson was suspended for the bowl game after wrecking a teammate's car. Brewer, who had played most of the season at wide receiver, was quickly shifted back to tailback in time for the game against the home state school that had snubbed him.

THE GAME OF MY LIFE
BY RYAN BREWER

I was nervous right off the bat. It was Ohio State, and the first thing that hit me was, "What if I have a bad game? What if I go out there and don't perform?" And with what happened with Derek, I was the man on the spot.

Obviously, I was starting at receiver that whole year, but when Lou said I was starting at running back, I was loving it. I could play running back; that was my home position. But I had mixed emotions. Derek was a stud, no doubt about it. We needed him to win that game, but I wanted to be able to tote the rock.

Lou was nervous about playing me. He was hoping that I would shine. He knew I had the motivation, but he also knew I had a lot of nervous energy, too. Warming up before the game, they pitched the ball and it was low and I dropped it. He got on me, and that kind of settled me down and got me ready to go for the game.

We watched the movie *Gladiator* the night before the game. On that first kickoff, I said, "Unleash hell." From the opening kickoff, I was going down smacking people. I was on all the special teams as well as playing tailback. I didn't want to come out of that game.

The other team talked trash to me the whole game. The first half, I was getting beat up and they were grabbing things they shouldn't have grabbed: not just my facemask, but whatever they could get their hands on. I knew a lot of their players from high school. The more they talked, however, the angrier they made me, and the better I played.

Offensively, you could tell that their defense had never seen the speed our offensive line had. We had guys who could move. I was getting a bunch of carries during the first half, but we weren't really moving the ball. We came in at halftime leading 3-0. I found out later that Coach was close to pulling me out of the game.

But the more carries I got, the better I felt, and things started going from there. We just kept running the toss sweep where the guards were pulling, where I had the option to stretch the defense or cut back.

We were pounding at them the whole time but we couldn't get in the end zone. We got down close, and Andrew Pinnock missed a block on a running play. He came up and told me, "I won't miss this time. You're going to score." Andrew drilled the guy. He put the guy on his back, and I pretty much walked into the end zone for our first touchdown. I felt then like we'd broken the ice, and we were ready to go.

I started touching the ball more and more. They just tried to get the ball in my hands a little more. That's what Lou did when he felt like a guy had the hot hand. It got to the point in that game where nothing mattered; Ohio State wasn't going to stop me. We got the ball in my hands and we made the thing work. I was in the zone. A lot of players talk about it, but that was the first time in college where I felt like there was no stopping me.

I was standing on the sideline as the clock was winding down, with us winning 24-7. I could feel my heart beating through my pads. Everybody was coming over and patting me on the back, hugging me. It was one of those feelings you never get back.

When I was being interviewed on the field by ESPN, Coach Cooper came up behind me and whispered in my ear, "Congratulations. I made a mistake, but I was a walk-on, too." I actually wasn't a walk-on, but at the moment, I just said, "OK, thanks, I appreciate it."

THE AFTERMATH

Ryan Brewer truly played the game of his life against Ohio State. He rushed 19 times for 109 yards and two touchdowns and caught three passes for 92 yards and a touchdown. Brewer was selected the game's Most Valuable Player for his performance.

However, South Carolina started out slowly. The Gamecocks had some success moving the ball in the first half, but couldn't push the ball into the end zone.

Jason Corse kicked a 23-yard field goal for a 3-0 lead early in the second quarter, but he also missed a 34-yarder.

Fortunately for the Gamecocks, their defense was giving the Buckeyes all they could handle, and South Carolina went in at halftime leading 3-0.

South Carolina finally got rolling late in the third quarter thanks to a setup from its defense. Gamecock nose tackle Cleveland Pinckney recovered a Buckeyes fumble at the Ohio State 28-yard line. Seven plays later, Brewer scored on a 7-yard touchdown run to put South Carolina ahead 10-0.

Ohio State then drove 66 yards with Mike Gurr recovering a fumble by Jonathan Wells in the end zone for a Buckeyes touchdown that cut the Gamecocks' lead to 10-7.

The fourth quarter was all South Carolina, with Brewer scoring on a 28-yard screen pass from quarterback Phil Petty and adding a 2-yard touchdown run with 7:10 left to play for the final score that put the Gamecocks ahead 24-7.

Ryan Brewer played two more years for the Gamecocks after his MVP performance in the Outback Bowl. Interestingly enough, he got another shot at the Buckeyes when Ohio State and South Carolina met again in the January 1, 2002 Outback Bowl.

South Carolina beat Ohio State 31-28, although Brewer did not play quite as big a role in the second victory over the Buckeyes.

Plagued by a severe ankle injury, Brewer's senior year was anticlimactic. But he gamely battled on, playing, as Holtz put it, "on one good leg."

After his playing career at South Carolina was over, Brewer signed a free agent contract with the Baltimore Ravens in 2003. One of the final players cut, he spent one season playing in NFL Europe before returning to Columbia to start a fencing business.

Brewer has fond memories of his playing career, particularly that first Outback Bowl team.

"It was as close knit as any team I've been on," he said. "We were all together. It wasn't offensive linemen together, running backs together, it was everybody together. That's the biggest thing about when I first came to South Carolina; I felt like it was a segregated team. Segregated by class, by position, by race, by everything. When our class came in, there was none of that at all."

Chapter 6

JEFF GRANTZ

THE YOUNG LIFE OF JEFF GRANTZ

Jeff Grantz was a natural. It didn't matter the sport—football, basketball, or baseball—he excelled in just about everything he tried.

Even so, Grantz held another trump card in his young athletic career that he believes was equally important. Grantz learned sporting fundamentals from his father, Chuck, a high school coach and athletic director, and he was also fortunate enough to grow up in a town where sports were important.

"It kind of came natural," Grantz said, "but I think a lot of it was because from early on I was taught the right way to throw the ball, how to run the ball."

The Bel Air, Maryland of Grantz's youth was a small community of approximately 10,000 people located just north of Baltimore, about five miles off Interstate 95.

"It was a growing area, a nice area outside of Baltimore," he said. "We played a lot of sandlot ball growing up in the neighborhood and I hung around with some older guys who played. I was fortunate to be in an environment that gave you an opportunity to learn.

"Even though the community was small, the high school was large because it drew from about a 10-mile radius in the county. There were a lot of great athletes."

One of those great athletes was Grantz, who particularly excelled at football and baseball.

Interestingly enough, he didn't play for his father.

When Jeff reached high school age, Chuck Grantz was coaching at Parkville High School, located approximately 16 miles away from Bel Air. Although Parkville had just started a football program, Chuck Grantz wanted to get the powerful Bel Air team, quarterbacked by his son Jeff, on the schedule.

"His team was actually the first team I ever started against as a sophomore," Jeff said. "We won the game handily, I didn't even play the second half. He just wanted to schedule Bel Air so he could show them what big-time high school football was all about. He wanted to let them know, 'This is what we're trying to get to.' I played against them all three years. We got them every time pretty good."

After those games, father and son would talk it over, with Chuck analyzing Jeff's game. By Jeff's senior year, there were plenty of college scouts around analyzing Jeff's game as well, and they liked what they saw.

Jeff wanted to play football and baseball in college, and was all but set to go to North Carolina, but told the Tar Heels he planned on one more visit—to South Carolina.

"I came down and looked everything over, and they said I could play both, so South Carolina is where I decided to go," Grantz said.

THE SETTING

During Jeff Grantz's freshman year, South Carolina ran a pro-style offense with drop-back passer Bill Troup as the starting quarterback.

But then the Gamecocks made a switch to the veer, an option-style offense that was all the rage in the 1970s. It was a bad fit for Troupe, who transferred. But it was a perfect fit for Grantz, who was destined to excel.

Grantz missed winter workouts during his freshman year because he was concentrating on baseball. When spring practice rolled

Jeff Grantz. *Photo provided by Collegiate Images/South Carolina*

around, he tried to keep up with both football and his baseball responsibilities.

"I went through a football scrimmage one Saturday afternoon, then came back out in my baseball uniform for a night game against Clemson," Grantz recalls. "I got a base hit and we beat Clemson. It was the best sporting day I've ever had in my life."

Because he missed winter workouts, Grantz started out sixth on the depth chart at quarterback. However, by the end of spring, Grantz was penciled in as the starter, and his spectacular three-year run as the Gamecocks' starting quarterback was about to begin.

Grantz was a natural fit in the veer offense, and it came easily to him since his high school also had run an option attack.

"Basically, the veer works when the offensive linemen are able to knock the defense off the ball one yard," Grantz said. "They're not necessarily making holes, but just moving the line of scrimmage one yard to give the quarterback the opportunity to read and operate down the line. That's when you can put the ball in the belly [of the fullback] and read the tackle. But if there's penetration, it's very difficult to read. So if the quarterback can make correct reads, it's a pretty potent offense."

South Carolina's offensive line knew how to block, and Grantz knew how to read it.

When the Gamecocks played Ohio University in Grantz's sophomore year, the Bobcats decided they would cover the dive and the pitch and make Grantz beat them running the football.

Grantz rushed for 260 yards, and South Carolina won 38-22. For good measure, he had an 80-yard kickoff return for a touchdown.

"It was just open for me to run it just about every time," Grantz said. "They never adjusted. Now that was fun."

By the time Grantz was a senior, head coach Paul Dietzel had been replaced by Jim Carlen.

Led by Grantz, two talented running backs named Kevin Long and Clarence Williams, wide receiver Phillip Logan, and a veteran offensive line, the Gamecocks were poised for a big year.

THE GAME OF MY LIFE
BY JEFF GRANTZ

Even though I'm from Maryland, I knew the importance of the rivalry with Clemson. It became important to me immediately because when I made my official visit to South Carolina, they were playing Clemson at Williams-Brice Stadium. The quarterback for South Carolina that day threw six interceptions. That was when I was recruited, and I saw what the Carolina-Clemson rivalry was all about even before I was ever involved in it. I also saw the six interceptions and said, "Gosh, maybe I can play there."

We had a pretty good season going my senior year. We were 5-1, but then we lost at LSU, then got beat by N.C. State in the last minute and got upset by Appalachian State. That really stung. That left two games: Wake Forest and Clemson at home. We took care of business against Wake Forest, which we were supposed to do. Going into the Clemson game, we knew we had to beat them to go to a bowl game. That was the focus right there. We should have been in a bowl game by then anyway, but the last-minute loss to N.C. State followed by the Appalachian State upset put us in a bind.

Going in, we felt very prepared. Our offensive line felt like they could dominate the game, which they did. It was the best game they played all year. There was a lot of motivation to get Clarence Williams to a thousand yards. Kevin Long already had a thousand, and we wanted it for Clarence, too. And there was a sense of urgency because we had to win that game to get to a bowl.

We were on a mission, and the coaches put us in good position to beat Clemson. Actually, they put in a wrinkle on offense where we would put a running back in motion, which we had not done all year. One of the reasons we were so successful at throwing the ball was because that man in motion screwed up their coverage; they never adjusted to it. When we needed a first down or a big play, we put Clarence Williams in motion and they didn't adjust. Four of the five touchdown passes I threw that day came off that man in motion.

We just rolled that day, in control from start to finish. I know they were upset by our last touchdown. That play happened to be a fourth and goal from about the 20-yard line. I called an out pattern to our split end. He broke fairly open, but I threw a low and outside ball and he made a diving catch in the end zone. Is that running it up? Yeah, maybe I should have kneeled on the ball, but I was into the game. I called the play at the line of scrimmage; it was my last home game, I was going to try to score. I felt that trying to kick a field goal would have felt more like running up the score. I can see how the other team felt, but I still don't regret that touchdown. I didn't have to play them anymore. So there it was, 56-20. It was a great win for us and it was the end of a great, fun career.

THE AFTERMATH

Grantz saved his best for his last home game, and it was a heck of a swan song.

He rushed for 122 yards and a touchdown and passed for five touchdowns, and South Carolina's offense rolled up 616 yards in total offense in a 56-20 victory.

Clarence Williams, who entered the game needing 113 yards to get to 1,000 for the season, finished with 160. He got the game off to a good start for the Gamecocks by scoring on a 36-yard run on South Carolina's opening drive of the game.

On the Gamecocks' next possession, Grantz threw for the first of his five touchdowns, a 34-yarder to Randy Chastain.

South Carolina's next three drives all ended with touchdown passes from Grantz to Phil Logan, covering 13, 41, and three yards.

Clemson was never in it. The Tigers trailed 35-6 at the half, and the Gamecocks just kept pouring it on. South Carolina never had to punt, scoring on nine consecutive possessions, although one touchdown was called back because of a penalty.

Grantz scored on a 19-yard run in the third quarter to put South Carolina ahead 49-12.

The Gamecocks' final touchdown came with 54 seconds to play on a 19-yard touchdown pass from Grantz to Stevie Stephens.

The last South Carolina touchdown upset Clemson coach Red Parker, who vowed to never forget it.

Indeed, Parker did not.

The Tigers beat the Gamecocks 28-9 the next year at Clemson, and the Tigers were trying to add another score when time ran out.

The much-anticipated bowl bid came South Carolina's way notlong after the victory over Clemson, a matchup against Miami of Ohio in the Tangerine Bowl in Orlando, Florida.

The game proved a bit anticlimactic for Grantz and the Gamecocks, who never got on track offensively and lost 20-7.

Grantz was drafted in the 17th round by the Miami Dolphins, but that didn't work out.

"The Dolphins drafted me as an athlete," Grantz said. "They already had Bob Griese, Don Strock, and Earl Morrall at quarterback. I went down to their three-day mini-camp and they looked at me as a receiver. But I just didn't enjoy it. I wasn't comfortable as a receiver. When I got back, I never did sign."

Grantz came back to Columbia, South Carolina, where he resides to this day.

He worked as a graduate assistant coach at South Carolina for two years under head coach Jim Carlen. From there, Grantz worked for two years in the sporting goods industry before beginning a 23-year-long career with Budweiser. Presently, he works for Capitol Wine and Beverage, which distributes Coors products.

Grantz was inducted into the University of South Carolina Athletic Hall of Fame in 1985 and into the State of South Carolina Athletic Hall of Fame in 1988. Most of his passing records have since been broken, but he is still widely remembered as the best quarterback in South Carolina history.

In 2004, *The State* newspaper in Columbia polled its readers to select the greatest quarterback in South Carolina history. Grantz was the winner.

"That was special," Grantz said. "I was fortunate to have a good career, and I'm glad people still remember me."

Chapter 7
ALEX HAWKINS

THE YOUNG LIFE OF ALEX HAWKINS

Alex Hawkins has a simple explanation as to why he gravitated toward athletics while growing up in Charleston, West Virginia.

"There was absolutely nothing else to do," Hawkins said. "I had an older brother and from the time I was walking, I was swinging a bat or something. He was four years older than I was. We grew up with sports. What else were you going to do? We never had a car to go anywhere where there might have been more going on."

Hawkins proved to be a natural athlete, excelling at football and baseball, although basketball was his best sport in high school.

Scholarship offers in basketball came pouring in from 23 different schools, including big-time programs such as Kentucky and Indiana.

"I had a guy from Kentucky who came up to me and said, 'You can play basketball or football or both if you come to Kentucky,'" Hawkins remembers. "He said, 'We'll give you $200 a month, clothes, and we'll give you a farm.' I never asked him what kind of farm or what size. I just said, 'I don't want to be a farmer. That's out.' Back then, everybody was paying."

Even though he was highly recruited, Hawkins didn't see much of a future in basketball.

"I shot a two-handed set shot," he said. "The best player on our team had a jump shot. I never could master the jump shot, but I could see it was coming and I was going to be out of business with a two-handed set shot."

Hawkins' football fortunes turned around once he earned MVP honors in the state high school all-star game.

Most of the locals thought Hawkins would do the logical thing and sign with the West Virginia Mountaineers. But Hawkins had other ideas.

"It's a backwards state," Hawkins said. "I hate to say that, living in South Carolina, because it's not the most progressive state either. West Virginia has some of the nicest people in the world, but it was a shrinking state when I was there. My neighbors both played college football and they suggested, 'Get the hell out of West Virginia.' As I recall, there were about four million people living in West Virginia in 1955 and now there are less than two million. So everything was contracting even then. We had our 33rd high school reunion in Florida because there were more people living in Florida than in West Virginia.

"During the war years, there was plenty of work there and that's when I grew up. My father was a union worker, an electrician. It was a thriving state, but coal mining declined and timber declined, and it was going the wrong way."

One of the schools recruiting Hawkins' services was the University of South Carolina. One trip south was enough to convince Hawkins.

"They took me water skiing with this really pretty girl," he said. "I was thinking, 'clean air, clear water, and pretty girls.' West Virginia had none of the three, so I decided South Carolina was the place for me. I never did see that girl again, though."

Alex Hawkins. *Photo provided by Collegiate Images/South Carolina*

THE SETTING

When Hawkins arrived on the South Carolina campus, one of the first people he met was a halfback from Laurens, South Carolina, named King Dixon.

It would be hard to find two more disparate personalities. Hawkins was an unabashed free spirit, happy go lucky to a fault. Dixon was regimented, disciplined, almost military in his bearing. But the two would become the best of friends and would form one of the best running back tandems in school history, and the cornerstone of the Gamecocks' football teams from 1956-58.

"He'd laugh at me, and I'd laugh at him," Hawkins said. "We're completely different but still the best of friends. He was living the life he needed to live and I was, too. He never tried to convert me, and I damn sure didn't try to convert him.

"It was a running joke because Weems Baskin was the junior varsity coach and he used to kid that we could beat the varsity. We could have played them a good game. We had a lot of talent. I think we had nine players who would go on to play pro ball either in the NFL or Canada. So we had plenty of talent."

But before Dixon and Hawkins' sophomore year, the winds of change blew across the South Carolina campus.

Coach Rex Enright, who had recruited Hawkins to South Carolina with promises of clothes, cars, and cash, had moved into the athletic director's job.

Replacing him was a young assistant from Maryland named Warren Giese. When he arrived, Giese made it abundantly clear that the extra benefits would immediately cease.

"When he came in, that was it," Hawkins said. "No more extras. He said there were 51 or 52 players who were getting more than the NCAA will allow and it [was] going to stop. He said, 'If you can't live with that, write down the name of three schools that you'd like me to contact.' I quickly put down Texas, Kentucky, and Oklahoma. I went back to West Virginia that summer and waited for those schools to contact me. It got to be July, so I called Giese, and he said,

'Nobody has contacted you? That's really surprising.' I don't think he ever called."

So Hawkins remained at South Carolina, and entering his senior year, expectations were high for the Gamecocks.

South Carolina opened the season with an 8-0 victory over Duke, and was then scheduled to travel to New York to take on Army.

THE GAME OF MY LIFE
BY ALEX HAWKINS

We get to New York to play Army, and people were really playing the game up as a battle between me and their halfback, Pete Dawkins, their star player who would go on to win the Heisman that year. The headlines in the papers read "Hawkins vs. Dawkins." They were a really good football team with something like four All-Americans. I remember going out for the coin toss with Dwight Keith, who was the center and who was 6-2, maybe 205 pounds. Dixon weighed about 165 to 170. I weighed 175 or something like that. We met their captains, who were Bob Anderson, who was about 6-2, 250, and Pete Dawkins about the same—muscular legs and the whole thing. We shook hands for the coin flip.

As we walked back to the sideline, I said, "Did you see those sons of guns? Dang, they're going to kick our butts!"

Dixon said, "Don't start with that."

I said, "But did you see them? They're bigger than our offensive linemen are. Look at you, look at me, look at Dwight, for God's sake."

They used the lonesome end, which is just a flanker split out wide, but it had never been used much in college football. We only had one defense and it was a 5-4 defense.

We were all lined up over here, and they had a guy uncovered over there. It was their first game of the season so we hadn't seen any film on them. We had already played a game, so they had our film and knew that we only had one defense.

I sort of looked at the guy out there, and then, looking back at Dixon and knowing how regimented he was, I just knew it wasn't going to be good. I looked at him out there and he didn't even go in the huddle. They would signal him what plays they were going to do. The first play, they threw it to him and we chased him about 20 yards and made the tackle. He didn't even go back in the huddle. They threw it to him again, and again, and it took about three or four plays and he scored.

I said, "King, you're going to have to go out there."

He said, "No, no, you don't understand. You turn the play in and I'll make the tackle."

"No, you don't understand," I said. "It ain't going to be but this one play if we don't get somebody out there."

I went to assistant coach Ernie Lawhorne and said, "We've got to get another defense. Somebody has got to get out there."

"We haven't got but one defense," he said.

"Well, make up something," I said. "This is going to be a long afternoon."

We never adjusted. 45-8. It could have been worse, but they took mercy and started running the ball. It was such a butt kicking, that's why it was so memorable to me. I'd never been beaten like that, ever. We weren't even in the game.

THE AFTERMATH

Earl "Red" Blaik's Army team did indeed administer a whipping of the first order on the Gamecocks.

The Black Knights completed 15 of 25 passes against the Gamecocks, which in those days, was really filling the air with footballs. Many of the completions came from "the lonesome end" formation.

At halftime, Army led 19-0 and had piled up 253 yards in total offense to South Carolina's 45.

Army did indeed take it easier on the Gamecocks in the second half, substituting liberally. Dawkins scored four touchdowns and halfback Bob Anderson passed for two.

Army led 38-0 before South Carolina finally drove 52 yards and scored on a 1-yard touchdown run by quarterback Bobby Bunch with 7:50 left to play.

Hawkins rushed for the two-point conversion.

The setback at Army did not prevent Hawkins and the Gamecocks from going on to have a respectable season. South Carolina would finish the year 7-3 and ranked 15th in the final Associated Press poll. Hawkins was selected a third-team All-American by the Associated Press and Atlantic Coast Conference Player of the Year.

In two of his three seasons, Hawkins led the Gamecocks in receiving, while in another he led the team in rushing and passing. While that would seem to speak to his versatility, Hawkins maintains it says more about the Gamecocks' offense.

"We didn't have a quarterback, and if we had a quarterback, he didn't fit the system because Giese's system was very simplistic," Hawkins said. "It was three yards and a cloud of dust. He had been on a national championship staff at Maryland, so he saw no reason to change. It worked for them, but we had some damn good players. We had plenty of wide receivers, but we didn't have a pass play.

"We played really dull football. Dreadful. I was the leading passer and receiver. We only had one pass play, and that was the halfback option. So I would throw to Dixon and catch from Dixon. Giese was just doing what he knew to do and something that had been successful for him. But I was sitting there with a strong opinion on everything. Still that way."

Hawkins went on to a 10-year NFL career, mostly with the Baltimore Colts.

Never a star, Hawkins' versatility earned him a spot on the Colts' roster. He served as a backup wide receiver, a tailback, and a special teams member. It was his work on special teams that earned him the endearing nickname "Captain Who."

"Don Shula decided he was going to have a special teams captain, and I was it," Hawkins said. "John Unitas was offensive captain and Gino Marchetti was defensive captain. I went out for the first time, and the referee greeted Unitas and Marchetti. I said, 'I'm Captain Hawkins,' and he says, 'Captain who?'"

Once he retired, Hawkins' career and his off-the-field exploits proved fertile ground for his autobiographical tale, *My Story and I'm Sticking To It*.

Renowned sports writer Dan Jenkins reviewed it thusly: "Merely the funniest damn book that ever got wrote by an ex-athlete his ownself."

Hawkins wrote a sequel, *Then Came Brain Damage* and more recently has authored two cookbooks, filled with popular recipes for tailgating.

Retired and living in a house above the Edisto River near Denmark, South Carolina, Hawkins spends most of his time playing golf and fishing.

And, of course, he still follows the Gamecocks.

Chapter 8

KING DIXON

THE YOUNG LIFE OF KING DIXON

When World War II broke out, King Dixon's father joined the Navy, leading to a life on the move in his early years. The family lived in Miami, Norfolk, Brookline, Massachusetts, and Staten Island, New York, as well as in Nova Scotia, following their Navy father from port to port. Eventually, the Dixon family settled in Laurens, South Carolina, where King's paternal grandmother had relocated to oversee a string of ice plants in rural Georgia and South Carolina.

Through his time in the Navy, Dixon's father came to know many of that era's biggest college sports names in the South, including Clemson coach Frank Howard and Georgia coach Wally Butts as well as Duke All-America tailback Ace Parker and Bill Murray, who led Duke to seven Atlantic Coast Conference championships from 1953 to 1965.

A star athlete at Laurens High School who set the state record in the 100-yard dash in just over 10 seconds, Dixon was pursued by most every major school in region and beyond. He already had won appointments to the Air Force and Naval academies as well as to West Point.

But Dixon, who wanted to be a doctor, signed with Duke during the spring of his senior year. A short time later he was invited to take a tour of the medical school in Durham, North Carolina, where he and a group of students, including a handful of athletes, watched doctors clean the gangrene out of the stump of a man's leg, which had been cut off at the knee.

"The blood was dripping down into a bucket and gauze was going in and tourniquets were being put on and the ether was coming up. My whole life went before me watching that," Dixon said. "I literally turned and ran out of that room as fast as I could and threw up outside. None of the coaches were there. They probably found out about it.

"But shortly thereafter I sent a note to Coach Murray that said I [was] no longer interested in becoming a medical doctor. I cannot handle that."

At about this time, Dixon's father was elected to the state House of Representatives, which led the younger Dixon to calculate that it was probably smart for him to go to South Carolina or Clemson.

Frank Howard came hard after the Laurens High School Tiger star—or "Kingy Boy," as Howard called him. As Dixon pondered his choices, Howard sent him a telegram that read: "King, you have been an outstanding Tiger for four years. Don't fowl up today. Your coach, Frank Howard."

But Dixon turned Howard down for Rex Enright and the Gamecocks, which of course didn't set well with Howard.

Dixon remembers Howard's words: "Kingy Boy would have come up here with the Tigers, but they promised down there in Columbia they was going to make his daddy governor if Kingy Boy went down there."

Dixon recalls, "Coach Howard said, 'Hell, he couldn't get the majority of votes in his family and there are only three of them.' It's that kind of relationship I had with Coach Howard."

THE SETTING

Dixon was part of a strong freshman class—including Dixon's future running mate, Alex Hawkins. But Enright would never get to coach them—freshmen were ineligible—because he was gone after South Carolina finished 3-6 in 1955.

After the season, Enright was replaced by Warren Giese, who was considered one of the keys behind the national titles Maryland won under Jack Tatum. With Giese running a split-T on offense and a defense called "The White Cloud," the Gamecocks finished 7-3 in 1956 and 1958.

In between, in 1957, South Carolina was a disappointing 5-5.

"My first game I actually earned a game ball," Dixon said of South Carolina's 26-13 victory over Wofford on September 15, 1956. "I still have that ball."

The next week South Carolina won 7-0 over Duke, which had a quarterback by the name of Sonny Jurgensen, who went on to star in the NFL. It was South Carolina's first win over the Blue Devils since 1931.

With back-to-back 13-0 wins over Maryland and Wake Forest to end the season, optimism was running high in Columbia as 1957 rolled around. But the Gamecocks lost their opener to Duke, 26-14. They then beat Wofford 26-0 and were headed to Austin to take on the big, bad Texas Longhorns in what would be the first—and so far, only—game between the two schools.

In a stunning turn of events, the Gamecocks beat Texas 27-21.

THE GAME OF MY LIFE
BY KING DIXON

If you ever play the Longhorns out there in Texas, and you line up there and those fired-up Texans sing the "Eyes of Texas are Upon You," you know you are in a different world. It's a great, wonderful setting for a football game. Of course, when we showed up and got off the bus, we were so small compared to the Longhorns that I think they thought we were the glee club coming out there to sing.

While I was out there, I got hit with a case of diarrhea and I had a temperature; I didn't feel well at all. I told the coach, and the trainer treated me as best as he could. But I felt so bad I really didn't know whether or not I was going to play. That afternoon was a long one, waiting for that night game.

We had a tremendous team and we thought, with the talent that we had coming back from the 7-3 season, we were in a position to win this ACC championship.

Interestingly enough, I did play—I started. We received the opening kickoff and I ran it back 98 yards. I caught the ball, took off toward the right sideline, and at about their 20-yard line, I had to cut around their safety man. When I did, I had a mishap; I soiled my trousers. And we had just gotten brand new, tight white trousers.

In any event, I was out of wind, came off the field and everybody was jumping up and down. What a way to start the game! But I ran over to Coach and said, "Coach, can I put a cape on?" He asked for what reason.

I said, "I've soiled my britches."

He said, "What?"

I said, "I've got to get out of these." And shortly thereafter, I was under that cape, went all the way under the stands, cleaned myself up with the cape still on, and came back out.

At halftime it was 21-7, Texas. Going into the fourth quarter it was 21-7, Texas. We got a second burst of wind out there because of a couple of bad punts. We scored three touchdowns in that fourth quarter out there, where the "Eyes of Texas are upon you," and we beat Texas 27-21.

I will never forget the headline in the paper, which read, "When Hawk got mad, Texas got sad." Alex really had a great fourth quarter. We played off each other; he was the right halfback, and I was the left halfback. He was the cornerback, and I was the safety on his side of the field. So we were in tandem.

I don't know of a more thrilling game when it comes to being away from home and playing a team of that stature and quality. I had an opportunity to play for Coach Royal later, by the way, in the North-South game after I graduated. It meant a lot to me.

If you talk to folks who listened to that game on the radio—nobody traveled that much in those days—that game sticks out as one of the greatest games for Carolina because we came back and beat a formidable opponent.

And as Alex Hawkins said in his book, *Cooking with Coccky,* I embarrassed him pretty severely: "because of one King Dixon, the University of Texas has never invited us back."

THE AFTERMATH

While that was the highlight of a .500 season, Dixon said another game also sticks out for him—one he didn't play in because he hurt his knee. On November 23, North Carolina State came to Columbia and barely escaped with a 29-26 victory.

"I was on the sideline on crutches," Dixon said.

That may have been the only way to slow Dixon down. Along with football, Dixon also ran track—including the 100-yard dash—at South Carolina for Coach Weems Baskin.

"My goal was to run a 9.6 in college. I did. But it was in my senior year against Duke University, the first outdoor meet of the year. There was a gentleman from Duke—he also played football that year—named Dave Sime. He was an Olympian that year, too," Dixon said.

"I ran a 9.6. Dave Sime happened to run a 9.3 and tied the world outdoor record that day. You know the difference between a 9.6 and a 9.3—8 yards. How can you beat 8 yards? So I learned a lot.

"I never will forget Coach Baskin telling me, 'King, get your head up. Your personal goal was to run 9.6. You weren't running against Dave Sime. He pushed you to be the very best you can. And he did. And you reached your goal. Get your head up.'

"But you know you're in fast company."

Along with his athletic exploits, Dixon went through the U.S. Marines Platoon Leader's Class on campus. Being a Navy man, Dixon's father didn't have much use for the Marines, telling his son the United States would have won World War II "much sooner had the Navy not had to keep pulling the Marines off the island."

"But," Dixon said, "I took a shine to the Marines."

Dixon spent his first three years playing and coaching football for the Marines, though he says he didn't volunteer to do either.

"I was drafted," he said with a laugh. "And in the Marines. when you're told we will support you and the Marines will win, you say, 'Yes, sir.' I had not anticipated that, and it caused some frustration."

Eventually, Dixon ended up going to Vietnam on a 13-month tour with Company B of the First Reconnaissance Battalion. "It was an interesting experience," he said. "We were the ears and eyes of the Third Marine Amphibious Force."

Dixon spent 22 years in the Marines, rising to the rank of Lieutenant Colonel and earning numerous combat honors, including the Bronze Star.

"I thought about retiring after 10 years," he said. "Everybody was so anti-military and against war in Vietnam. Most of us at that period of time were rather naïve. We didn't realize there were all these demonstrations going [on] back home.

While at home, Dixon had a couple job interviews, but what "stayed in my craw," as he put it, was when people would tell him that, after serving his country and spending so much time in the military, he must be sick of it all—he must have been "ready to get out."

He says, "Well, I was very close to a lot of people in the military and proud of the military. Regrettably, the military's hands were being tied [in Vietnam]. ... It was awful, now in retrospect to see— a real waste, real waste."

After his mother was diagnosed with cancer, Dixon did retire and worked with the Laurens YMCA as a banker before returning to his university, first on the alumni association and then as athletic director.

As AD, Dixon oversaw South Carolina joining the Southeastern Conference, although initially he was instructed to see if there were any way the ACC would welcome back the school. South Carolina had left the ACC in 1970.

"I was told by dear friends in the ACC, 'King, you don't want to bring it up for a vote because the university will be embarrassed. It will not pass,'" Dixon said. "So we didn't push it."

There was also talk of a "mega-conference" of 24 teams, stretching from New York to Florida. But ultimately the school determined their biggest opportunity was the SEC.

"Boy, what an experience that was, to go into the SEC," he said, "and I take great pride in that. It was a great thing. That was a real highlight. Not only did it open our blinders, but it also raised our sights, both academically and athletically, to be a part of a formidable conference. It was interesting times. It really was."

Chapter 9

BRANDON BENNETT

THE YOUNG LIFE OF BRANDON BENNETT

Growing up in Taylors in rural upstate South Carolina, Brandon Bennett was always playing sports. His mother was one of 13 children, and her siblings—along with other relatives—lived nearby. So there were plenty of willing participants for Bennett to recruit for sports.

"It was one of those things where from the time we got up to the time we laid down we were playing some type of sport," Bennett said.

Bennett played football and basketball. He also worked on his leaping ability, which would come in handy down the road, by doing the long jump, triple jump, and high jump in track, as well as the hurdles at Riverside High School.

Bennett was good enough in basketball to receive scholarship offers from some schools, but a hoard of schools liked what they saw from him in football and track. Track was nice, but he loved football.

"Football was something I always liked to play but I just pretty much enjoyed playing with my cousins," he said. "I never really thought I could make some money out of it or I could go to college."

But football did just that. After rushing for more than 1,000 yards as a sophomore at Riverside, Bennett started receiving recruiting letters from South Carolina and Clemson, among others.

After rushing for more than 1,000 yards again as a junior and being touted as one of the nation's top prep running backs, the letters poured in. And they didn't stop after Bennett rushed for 2,226 yards as a senior.

Bennett considered Clemson, Nebraska, Tennessee, and South Carolina. His mother didn't have a good feeling about Tennessee coach Johnny Majors, and Nebraska was too far away. Bennett liked Clemson, but the Tigers wanted him to play defensive back—Bennett had also played free safety at Riverside—so they were nixed.

It was on to Columbia and the Gamecocks.

THE SETTING

Bennett had barely arrived on campus, however, when he was ready to make a quick exit. Bennett decided to get a head start on his college career, both academically as well as athletically, by going to both sessions of summer school in 1991.

"That was different," he said. "I come from being here in a small town in Taylors to going to South Carolina and pretty much being thrown out on my own because I'm now traveling, I'm going to classes, I'm away from my family."

Along with classes, the players would get together during the second session of summer school to work out. As fate would have it, Bennett was the only freshman early on amidst a corps of veterans.

"I always got by on just straight athletic ability in high school. I got down there and it was one of those things that now I'm looking at these big linebackers and big linemen and we're having to run and it was like 100 degrees," he said.

"We came out there one day and the military had cancelled their workouts because they said there was a heat advisory. We're out there running and doing up and downs and whatever. I literally finished

Brandon Bennett. *Photo provided by Collegiate Images/South Carolina*

the run and I jogged back to the room and I was telling them I was quitting. It was too hot."

But some teammates, including his brother, Brayln, a wide receiver who lettered in 1990 and 1991, reassured the tired and confused Bennett that it would be all right, even if it would be different from high school.

"They kind of got me through it," Bennett said.

As a freshman, Bennett was penciled in behind hard-nosed Rob DeBoer, but as the weeks went on, Bennett earned more and more playing time. Ultimately, Bennett led the Gamecocks in rushing with 702 yards and nine touchdowns, the most ever by a South Carolina freshman.

The highlight of the season for Bennett came in a 55-7 win over East Tennessee State on October 5. Bennett rushed for a school-record 278 yards on 31 carries, scoring on runs of 1, 12, and 89 yards—the latter being the second-longest touchdown run in South Carolina history.

"I was worn out at the end of the game," he said. "I didn't have any sense it would be a special day because they were putting me in and taking me out. The thing that was funny is that the first couple of games the only plays I was playing were goal line-type stuff. They liked me to dive over the top. That's how everything got going.

"I wouldn't play throughout the field but I'd come in on goal line and dive over the top, score the touchdown. It was just kind of one of those things where they'd say, 'Rob's going to get us there and you dive over the top.'

"Then Rob ended up getting beat up and they threw me in there. I started doing good from the get-go and then they were like, shoot, now we've got two backs that are able to play. They ended up putting Rob at fullback and me at tailback."

In high school, games like ETSU were the norm for Bennett, not a half-dozen carries and 30 or 40 yards a game.

"I was aggravated [before the ETSU game]. Having a game under 200 yards was crazy to me," he said. "But that right there, it was kind of an eye-opener. It just let me know I could play on this level."

It was more of the same for Bennett over the next two years, leading the Gamecocks in rushing in 1992 with 646 yards and 1993 with 853 yards. In 1993, he also became the first player in school history to have over 100 yards rushing and receiving when he ran for 127 yards and caught five passes for 129 yards in a 34-3 victory over Louisiana Tech on September 18.

But the Gamecocks struggled, earning losing records each year.

"Me and Toby Cates and Tony Watkins still talk about [how] we were not as bad as our record showed," Bennett said. "But it's like we could always find a way of losing and not to win. Something crazy would always happen."

Not, however, on a special afternoon Between the Hedges in Athens, Georgia, on September 4, 1993, when Bennett etched his name in Gamecock lore by leaping into the end zone with two seconds left for a season-opening 23-21 victory over Georgia.

THE GAME OF MY LIFE
BY BRANDON BENNETT

We were a veteran team. There was a lot of talking before the season. Toby Cates, Steve Taneyhill, Tony Watkins, and I felt like all of us had been there together long enough. It was time for us to make a statement. We were good enough to play; we just had to show it on the field. So we were very optimistic.

Driving down was cool, especially for me, because I was thinking about how my family and all my friends were going to be there. This was one of the games of the week everybody was talking about. Everybody was just ready to play.

The night before, I was up and I couldn't even sleep. Stanley Pritchett and I were sitting around talking and just going over stuff. I kept looking over my playbook because my mind was going to so many places that I was just using that to relax myself. We were talking and saying, "Hey, we've got an opportunity. We're playing one of the best teams in our conference and everything. We've got to win this game."

We went out there and the crowd was booing. Really, that just excited me. My whole thing was, they're booing now but we're going to have them standing on their feet in a little while. That was my whole mentality; you're going to boo me now, but you're going to watch me run a couple of plays and make something happen. You're going to admit, okay, this guy can play.

It was very hot. The trainers were telling us to keep drinking water; it was going to be a long day. The coaches were like, "Hey, we're going to give you the ball. So get ready to run it." I was excited because they wanted to run the ball, and they wanted me to do it.

Both teams were moving the ball. We were going back and forth, back and forth. I broke down the sideline and got hit. I spun out and another guy hit me. Then I fumbled the ball. But Toby Cates dived on it in the end zone. I was mad at myself, but at the same time, it was fate. We were going to win that day because that was one of the weirdest plays that could have happened: I got tackled and kicked the ball with my foot and it went into the end zone and we dived on it for a touchdown to go up 17-7.

But Eric Zeier was their quarterback, and he scrambled around and they went up 21-17 in the fourth quarter. We were thinking, we've let them creep back in here. But we had to keep on playing; we'd scored on them before.

At that point in the game, everybody was talking in the huddle. Taneyhill came in and he said, "Ya'll shut up. Just relax." He said, "Look here, we're going to go down there and we're going to score. We've been doing it all day. They're not better than us. Let's just take the ball down and score and go home and party."

We got down there. The last time we went into the huddle, Taneyhill said, "We don't have much time. Let's punch it in there, B. Come on, ya'll just open the hole and we're going to get in there." Everybody said, all right, we got it, we got it. I tried to go over the top. But their defense grabbed me and pulled me back.

Taneyhill was yelling, "Just run it again!" They were trying to hold me down. But I got away and we lined up again. He called the same play, went through the cadence. It was blocked perfectly. If you watch it, you'll see that nobody is standing up in the whole play. The linemen got everybody down and I just dove over the top to get in there.

I knew it would be the last play. I had looked up at the clock. I was thinking, we've got to hurry up and get set. So we ran and got set up because we all knew then this was the last play. And I went over the top. They kind of stopped me a little, but then I flipped over to make sure I got in there.

THE AFTERMATH

As it turned out, that victory win was the highlight of the year. The Gamecocks would win only three more games, finishing 4-7 and spelling the end for coach Sparky Woods. Woods was replaced by Brad Scott, offensive coordinator for Florida State's 1993 national championship team.

"Everybody's looking at where [Brad Scott] was coming from and thinking, 'Okay, this guy has got to be good,'" Bennett said. "At that time everybody was like, okay, we're ready to play now. We've got great players. The only problem with us is we don't know how to win. Now we've got somebody here that knows how to win."

And win the Gamecocks did, finishing 7-5 in 1994 and beating West Virginia 24-21 in the Carquest Bowl, the first bowl win in school history. And while Bennett was happy to be part of that victory, it was "an up and down year" for him.

"We were going to the shotgun and throwing the ball. I was like, man, he's pretty much taken me out of the game plan," Bennett said. "We kind of bumped heads a couple times going over stuff about me not understanding what was going on and him trying to explain it. It was a trying year. We got to where it was okay. But I don't think we ever got to where we were buddies. It was hard."

Bennett tore his abdominal muscles in the bowl game and wasn't picked up in the NFL draft. He felt lost. He didn't know what the future held. He had gone from thinking he would be one of the top backs in the draft to wondering if his career was over.

He went to training camp with Cleveland as a free agent, but the Browns cut him. Then he spent the next couple years on the practice squads with Chicago and Miami. And then he got a chance to play at Cincinnati, where he spent eight years. After one year with the Charlotte Panthers, Bennett retired.

Looking back on his career, Bennett said he's glad he didn't give up on his dream of playing in the NFL—his 1,127 yards for the Bengals ranks 20th in team history. And despite a few rough spots, he enjoyed his time at South Carolina.

"I had a good time. They told me that they were going to let me come and play. They did that. I got an education. I wished I would have had the opportunity to run the ball a lot more," he said. "But all in all, I have no regrets."

Chapter 10

ANTHONY WRIGHT

THE YOUNG LIFE OF ANTHONY WRIGHT

Anthony Wright grew up in a town of less than 1,000 people that was named for former North Carolina Governor J.B. Vance. Vanceboro is a community about 25 miles east of East Carolina in Greenville, North Carolina. It is a blue-collar town, a community of hard-working and hardy people who farm and fish, and who work at various industrial companies, such as Moen, where Wright's mother worked as a supervisor, and DuPont, where his father was a machine operator.

Wright, born on Valentine's Day in 1976, sprang from this soil.

"I grew up in a tight-knit family. Father and mother talked about respect, obeying your parents and whatnot," Wright said. "I was just a country boy from North Carolina who loved to compete in everything I did, whether it was athletics or academics. I was just a competitor at heart."

Wright grew up idolizing NBA and North Carolina basketball star Michael Jordan, "another Eastern North Carolina boy himself," although Jordan grew up some three hours south of Vanceboro, in Wilmington. But what are a few hours when it comes to a boyhood idol?

As a youngster, Wright played everything, although football was his first organized sport. One day when Wright was about seven years old, his father was at the grocery store talking to the local football coach about what he could do to burn off some of his son's boundless energy.

"The coach just said, 'Bring him to me out there and let him get rid of some of that energy,'" Wright said. "So that's how it started."

Wright wasn't initially a quarterback. Taller than most of his teammates, he played defensive end and tight end. But a few years later, his coach was looking for a volunteer to run the scout team at quarterback. Enter Wright's cousin, Bobby Cox.

"The coach was pretty much pleading for somebody to come out and play," Wright said. "My cousin kept pushing me, lifting me up out of my seat. And the coach went ahead and called me out there. Ever since then, I kind of stuck with it."

It was love at first snap.

"I liked it. I had the ball in my hand a lot…I liked the attention. And I liked to run around with the ball," he said. "I found myself doing magical things back there, getting out of tackles and making guys miss. It seemed like a lot of fun."

At West Craven High School, Wright continued to have fun, starting his final three years on varsity at quarterback and leading his team to the state playoffs each season. But although he was getting letters of interest from colleges across the south, Wright said he wasn't sure of his talents.

"[In] the town that I'm from, it's not a big thing as far as people grooming you and people showing you the potential you have," he said. "I was just playing ball."

But at the end of his junior year, Wright was at the local mall when someone came up to him with a football magazine that ranked him as the No. 3 quarterback prospect in the land, right behind Peyton Manning and Josh Booty.

"It kind of surprised me," Wright said. "I wasn't doing this for that. I was just doing it because I liked to do it."

Anthony Wright. *Photo provided by Collegiate Images/South Carolina*

Wright actually took only one official recruiting visit—to South Carolina. He made unofficial trips to nearby ECU as well as North Carolina and North Carolina State. But his official visit to Columbia came on a day when the Gamecocks were playing archrival Clemson.

After that, Wright knew where he was going.

"Going to UNC or N.C. State or East Carolina, you might have a stadium filled with about 40,000 people," Wright said. "At South Carolina, it was 80,000. When I got there and saw that stadium with all those people, I was sold."

It also didn't hurt, Wright said, that South Carolina had just hired Florida State offensive coordinator Brad Scott as its new head coach. Wright had dreamed of playing for the Seminoles.

"He was going to run the Florida State offense," he said, "and I bit on it."

THE SETTING

Red-shirted as a freshman in 1994, Wright was willing to watch and wait—and learn. His big moment came in his first spring game, when offensive coordinator John Eason picked Wright to be his quarterback over senior Steve Taneyhill. Wright completed 17 of 28 passes for 242 yards and two touchdowns to lead his team to a 28-20 victory.

"A lot of the coaches actually picked at him about it," Wright said. "They were surprised he picked me. I remember him telling me that…and he wanted me to go out and show them why he'd picked me."

Wright spent 1995 behind Taneyhill, completing 17 of 27 passes for 207 yards and two touchdowns in limited action in nine games. As 1996 rolled around, Wright was the starter, replacing Taneyhill, who had graduated.

"I was definitely feeling pressure. I was a little nervous, a little anxious," Wright said. "I didn't know what to expect. There were a couple practices leading up to the first game where I just wasn't in sync mentally. The pressure had started to wear on me a little bit."

No wonder. As Wright prepared for his first college start against Central Florida on September 7, 1996, he also was making school history as the first African-American to start at quarterback—at least two others had played the position—for the Gamecocks in 104 years of football.

At the time, Wright said it wasn't something he had given a lot of thought. Scott had already faced this when Charlie Ward became the first African-American to start at quarterback for Florida State.

But a decade later looking back on that week, Wright said he downplayed the importance of the moment to ease the pressure.

"I needed to downplay it at that time," he said. "But now when I look back on it and realize the accomplishment and realize the struggle, it's definitely more gratifying to me that I was able to do that."

Wright performed well. He completed 12 of 19 passes for 236 yards, including a 53-yard touchdown to Marcus Robinson as the Gamecocks beat future NFL quarterback Daunte Culpepper and the Golden Knights 33-14.

A record crowd of 76,411 was on hand at the newly expanded Williams-Brice Stadium to see Wright's debut—and history made.

"The game moved a lot slower than I anticipated [given his pregame anxiety]," Wright said. "It helped build my confidence."

The next week, before a second straight record crowd South Carolina defeated Georgia 23-14 on ESPN.

"I thought that was the beginning of something real, real sweet," Wright said. Instead, the Gamecocks lost their next three games en route to a 6-5 season that ended without a bowl bid. In a rainstorm, South Carolina lost to ECU 23-7.

"There was more rain on the field than grass," Wright recalled.

Then the following week, Mississippi State won in Columbia 14-10 despite Wright throwing for 351 yards—only three quarterbacks in school history have thrown for more yards.

"I remember [MSU defensive coordinator] Joe Lee Dunn throwing about 900 blitzes at us, and we couldn't pick up any of them," Wright said. "The biggest question I have for the whole season is, how could I have thrown for 351 yards and scored only 10 points? I can't explain it. That was a game that was hard for us to swallow."

But there was more disappointment to come for Wright in 1997; his season ended prematurely with a severe knee injury. After beating Central Florida 33-31 in its opener, South Carolina lost at Georgia 31-15. But then came a homecoming of sorts for Wright.

The Gamecocks were headed to Greenville, North Carolina. With about 50 friends and family in the stands, Wright helped lead South Carolina to a 26-0 victory over ECU. "It's a game you dream about, to go back and play a team you basically grew up around," he said.

But then came two straight losses: at Mississippi State 37-17, and to Auburn 23-6. Wright and the Gamecocks could feel the season slipping away as Tim Couch and Kentucky rolled into town.

Not only were the Wildcats averaging 36.4 points and 473.8 yards total offense, but they were coming off a 40-34 overtime win against Alabama—their first victory over the Crimson Tide in 75 years.

It was not a great personal performance for Wright, who rushed for a career-high 63 yards but completed 15 of 24 passes for just 129 yards, including a 27-yard pass to Cory Bridges with 3:16 left in the game.

But in leading South Carolina from a 14-3 deficit to win 25-14, the game stands out for reasons far beyond numbers for Wright.

THE GAME OF MY LIFE
BY ANTHONY WRIGHT

At that particular time in the season for us, the guys were looking for answers. I remember saying to myself, if we're going to win games, then I was going to have to do everything I could to make sure that we won, and I was going to have to lead. And if the guys didn't follow me, they just didn't follow me. But I was going to have to take this and do it myself.

Then there was this article in the newspaper, questioning us. It wasn't really criticizing me; it was criticizing the team. But I took it personally because I was part of the team and part of that family. I have a competitive side and it was like wildfire. I wanted to start a fire with my team. I wanted people to play with their souls and their hearts and not just with their bodies. That's how we were going to win games.

I think in that particular game, that kind of thinking caught on. Initially, we weren't playing together as a team. We were still looking for somebody to step up and make something happen. I kind of asserted myself and showed I was going to give everything I had for the team. I think at that point it caught on like wildfire.

Once I saw that article, I had a chip on my shoulder. And when I went into that game, I still had a chip on my shoulder. I played like I wanted to prove everybody wrong. I wanted to prove to all the naysayers—the writers, everybody who was talking about Kentucky quarterback Tim Couch and about what he was going to do—that they were wrong.

Early on, we were down 14-3. The State Fair was going on at that time. People had started to leave and go to the Fair. People were booing. It was getting ugly, or it was about to get ugly anyway.

I remember saying to myself, "I'm going to take the game over." I broke four or five tackles running down the sideline. Then I fumbled the ball. As I fumbled, the ball bounced down the sideline, and I scooped it back up and ran for another 5 or 10 yards.

I shifted my game into overdrive. I was playing like I wasn't going to play any more football. I think that everybody else on the team caught on. Arturo Freeman caught a pick and ran it for a touchdown, and Jermale Kelly started coming on. He had a couple big touchdowns, and we won the game by 14 points against the great Tim Couch and Kentucky Wildcats and their great offense.

Statistically speaking, it might not have been my best game, but personally, that's the game I felt the best about. That was probably one of the best games I had in my career at USC.

THE AFTERMATH

The win was the first of three straight for the Gamecocks, who were 5-3 and on a roll as they headed to Knoxville to face No. 8 Tennessee. The Volunteers, favored by 21, won 22-7, but the story for Wright was a sad one.

His junior season was over. With 6:19 left in the second quarter, Wright, who had never suffered anything worse than a sprained ankle and wrist in football, tore ligaments in his right knee as he tried to twist out of a sack by linebacker Al Wilson.

"It was tough," he said.

Wright didn't take part in spring ball in 1998 but was ready to go when the Gamecocks began practicing for what would turn out to be a forgettable season—and Scott's last as head coach.

But that was still ahead. In the opener, South Carolina beat Ball State 38-20, and Wright completed his first eight passes and also had a 30-yard run.

"I remember that run," he said. "When I cut back across the field, my knee slipped on me. But it was one of those games that I was just happy to be back on the field and playing."

It was the highlight of the year. South Carolina would not win again, finishing 1-10. Five of those losses were by nine points or less.

"It's one of the worst things I've been through," Wright said. "That really hurt me emotionally, dealing with the fans and the whole situation and dealing with going 1-10, knowing all I had gone through to get back. But it's something that made me stronger for the future."

But what did the future hold?

Wright was invited to the NFL combine and did well. Then one day his agent called him after he returned to Columbia and asked him to meet him at his doctor's office where he told Wright that five or six teams were interested in picking him on the first day of the draft.

There was only one problem. Wright failed each team's physical because of his knee.

"I'm stunned. I'm like, what's going on?" he said. "[My agent] told me that a lot of guys failed me because my knee wasn't done properly in college; they hadn't tied my ACL down correctly."

Some teams were willing to draft him and have him undergo surgery again and put him on the injured reserve for a year. Wright didn't know what to do. Finally, figuring he'd already lasted an entire college season, he'd take his chances and not have the surgery.

The gamble didn't pay off. Wright wasn't drafted but did sign a free agent contract with Pittsburgh. He played so well during the preseason he forced the Steelers to keep four quarterbacks.

The next year he moved on to Dallas, where he spent two years, starting three games in 2001 before deciding to have his knee repaired again. Then it was on to Baltimore, where he spent four seasons, coming on in the second half of the 2003 season and helping lead the Ravens to five wins in seven games to clinch the AFC North.

After 2005, however, Wright signed with the Cincinnati Bengals, his fourth team in an eight-year NFL career that had seen him complete 55.1 percent of his passes for 3,547 yards and 20 touchdowns.

Wright knows there are plenty of people back in Columbia surprised at his NFL success.

"You don't stay in the league eight years doing nothing. People are not paying you just to hold a notebook. I'm pretty sure they are surprised. I think they're more surprised because of everything I'd been through down there," he said.

"A lot of the fans don't really understand what happened the last couple years I was down there. It was an unfortunate thing for the school and unfortunate thing for me, too. Things that happened in those years didn't really tell the truth about the talent we had. Me being the quarterback, I had to take responsibility for a lot of it."

Wright said he never doubted he would make it in the NFL.

"I knew it was just matter of somebody giving me a chance. I've been proving myself over and over in the NFL, time and time again," he said. "They're not giving me anything. I'm earning it. I've earned it for eight years."

And what of his years at South Carolina?

"Cut and dry, it was bittersweet. I found my wife from going to the University of South Carolina. That's always a good thing. I got an education," Wright said. "The '97 season was a decent season. But I never had any true winning season. So it was bittersweet.

"I went to South Carolina hoping that I could help change things, help bring a winning attitude to the program. But that didn't happen. So it was kind of disappointing. But other than that, though, things happen for a reason. If I hadn't gone to South Carolina, maybe I wouldn't be in the league [NFL] right now.

"Maybe if I had gone to North Carolina, we would have been running the option or whatnot, and I wouldn't have known what cover two was, or what cover three was, or cover six or cover eight or cover zero. So everything happens for a reason. At the end of the day, things being the way they are, I'm happy. I can't complain. I've been blessed."

Chapter 11

MIKE HOLD

THE YOUNG LIFE OF MIKE HOLD

When Mike Hold was a freshman in high school, he stood 5 feet tall and weighed 85 pounds, but a lack of size did not prevent him from venturing into the world of competitive sports.

From a young age, Hold played football, soccer, baseball, and also wrestled. He was good at all of them, and pursued sports with a passion.

"I remember always having a ball, or a ball and a bat," he said. "It was always athletics. Back then, we didn't know what computers were, so that's all we did. It was always outdoors and sports. We actually moved to California when I was in kindergarten, [staying there] through fifth grade, and Pop Warner football was huge. I played two years of Pop Warner and then we moved back to Phoenix. Then my dad didn't want me to play. The reason being is he didn't want me to burn out. He wanted me to continue to do everything. So I actually played soccer for a couple years.

"It wasn't like football was the only sport by any means. Wrestling was my favorite sport. In high school, I played football, baseball, and I wrestled."

Fortunately for Hold's football future, a growth spurt of sorts ensued, and by his senior year, he was 5-foot-8 and 150 pounds.

That size still wasn't enough to draw attention from major college scouts, even though Hold did lead his team to the state championship his senior year.

"I didn't get a sniff from major college coaches," Hold said, "but I got one JUCO offer and that was from Mesa Community College."

Hold excelled at Mesa, and—equally important to his future—the growth spurt continued.

After two years, he had grown to a shade under six feet, and so finally started to attract the attention of a few college coaches.

One of those coaches was Joe Lee Dunn, an assistant coach at New Mexico who was elevated into the head coaching position when Joe Morrison left New Mexico to take the South Carolina job in 1983.

Morrison wanted to run the veer at South Carolina, and as luck would have it, Hold's Mesa team had converted to an option offense late in his second season at just about the time Dunn began to scout him.

Dunn called his old buddy Morrison to tell him about Hold.

"He called Coach Mo and said, 'You need to take a look at this guy,'" Hold said. "I was actually visiting Oklahoma as a kicker when I got a call that South Carolina had called and wanted me to come out for a visit. I didn't know anything about South Carolina. They told me it was where George Rogers, the guy who won the Heisman Trophy [in 1980] was from. In my heart of hearts, I wanted to go to Arizona State, but they weren't interested."

Hold remembers having a great time on his visit to South Carolina, but he came home and told his parents that he wanted to walk on at Arizona State.

"They said, 'OK, but if you turn down a scholarship to do that, you've got to pay for your own school,'" Hold said. "That's what I was going to do, but when [assistant coach Frank] Sadler called and wanted to know what I was going to do, I just said, 'I'm coming.' I just couldn't tell him no. I wasn't 100 percent sure I was doing the right thing, but that's how it happened. It was the best decision I've ever made in my life."

Mike Hold. *Photo provided by Collegiate Images/South Carolina*

THE SETTING

For a kid who had spent all his life in Arizona and California, moving to South Carolina provided a bit of culture shock. Hold almost didn't survive it.

"I made two Ds and a B my first semester," he said. "I was trying to get out so bad. I remember saving up my money so I could come home for spring break. But once I came back from the break, I kind of settled in and started making friends."

Hold ultimately suffered a knee injury that led to a redshirt year in 1983, and as preparations began for the 1984 season, he appeared to be penciled in as a backup to starting quarterback Allen Mitchell.

Hold didn't play in the Gamecocks' season-opening victory over The Citadel, and only sparingly in a mop-up role the next week against Duke.

"I was kind of a loosey-goosey type of guy," Hold said. "You know, kind of a California guy. It drove Coach Sadler insane, even though it was just my way of coping with nerves. He came up to me after a practice and said, 'As long as I'm offensive coordinator you will never play here.' I went and called my dad and said, 'I'm coming home.' He said, 'All right, but do me one favor—stay one more week. You're in practice, you owe it to the team to at least do that.'"

The next game was against 12th-ranked Georgia, and fate would intercede in a big way for Hold's future and that of the 1984 Gamecocks.

Hold was languishing on the South Carolina bench when Mitchell suffered an arm injury against the Bulldogs with three minutes remaining in the third quarter and the score tied at 10.

Thrust into the action, Hold's first contribution was a third-down, quick-kick punt that covered 66 yards and bailed the Gamecocks out of poor field position. With 10:41 left to play in the game, South Carolina took over on its own 22-yard line.

Hold drove the Gamecocks down the field for the go-ahead score, completing a 62-yard pass to Ira Hillary and ultimately scoring the touchdown himself on a two-yard run.

South Carolina held on to win 17-10, and Hold's performance sparked the beginning of a two-quarterback system for the Gamecocks in 1984.

Two games later, the 5-0 Gamecocks headed to South Bend, Indiana, to take on Notre Dame.

THE GAME OF MY LIFE
BY MIKE HOLD

I just remember the hunger to win, to prove that the five prior wins were not a fluke, how big that win would be for us if we could get it. We had won five in a row at home, and this was our first road trip.

When you look at the whole season, it was kind of a pivotal game. Up until then, I don't think we were being respected. Even though Notre Dame was not the Notre Dame of old, it was still a good football team with excellent talent. They had guys like Steve Buerlein at quarterback and Mark Bavaro at tight end. For us to go in and win opened the nation's eyes. There were just so many things about that game that made it a big game for me, for the team: everything from the national attention to just winning at Notre Dame amidst all their tradition. That's an awesome place to go into, and to win was great for morale; it pushed us through the rest of the season.

The biggest play of the game for me came in the fourth quarter when we were trailing 26-22. I wouldn't call myself a runner. I'm more of a scrambler, and I had a 30-something-yard scramble for a touchdown that gave us the lead. With that offense, we had to be able to run some because of the veer. Fortunately, I was able to make a play.

I don't remember if it was that series, but I had gotten hit on the knee—it was a little sore. The guys in the huddle said, "Maybe you should go out." But I wasn't going to take myself out.

I don't remember specifics as far as down and distance. I just dropped back and all of a sudden it was just like the parting of the

Red Sea. It was just wide open. When I saw the opening, I instinctively took off. I remember getting a couple good downfield blocks. It just seemed like there was space and it wasn't closing up. I kept going and was able to get in.

I remember the feeling when the clock ticked off and we had won. When we got back to Columbia, there were thousands of fans waiting for us at the airport. It gives me chills to think about it right now. It was the most amazing thing I've ever been a part of. The people at the airport had lined up down the road. Danny Smith, one of the tight ends, climbed through a hatch in the roof of the bus and was sitting up there, screaming and hollering with the fans. It was an amazing scene and put into perspective what big-time football meant to that university. I don't want to talk too much about that one season being the greatest thing that ever happened, but when you look at it, it was amazing the way the town was in hysterics after that game. I think that game all of a sudden made everybody believers.

When you look back, we had to claw to beat The Citadel. So every game after that, it was like our winning was seen as a fluke. I think it really took that Notre Dame game to make everyone, including ourselves, realize that we might be for real. I think we grew as a team every game after that, believing in ourselves and keeping on the right track and continuing to win.

THE AFTERMATH

The Notre Dame game marked the second straight week that Hold's off-the-bench heroics saved the day for the Gamecocks.

South Carolina scored 22 points in the fourth quarter to beat the Irish 36-32. In addition to his 33-yard touchdown scramble, Hold scored on a one-yard run and led a drive that culminated in a four-yard touchdown run by Quinton Lewis.

Hold finished the game with 68 yards on 17 carries and completed four of nine passes for 66 yards.

The victory vaulted South Carolina from 11th to ninth in the next Associated Press poll, marking the first time in school history the Gamecocks cracked the top 10.

South Carolina would roll on to a 9-0 record and a No. 2 national ranking in 1984 before the bottom fell out in an inexplicable 38-21 loss at Navy that killed the Gamecocks' national title hopes.

The Gamecocks rebounded with a dramatic 22-21 victory against archrival Clemson, but lost 21-14 to a Jimmy Johnson-coached Oklahoma State team in the Gator Bowl.

Still, South Carolina's final record of 10-2 was the best in school history.

"I don't think we were as talented across the board as some teams, but I think we had more desire than any team we stepped on the field with," Hold said. "The one team that we were better than physically and were more talented than was Navy. I think we lost focus of what got us where we were. We had no business losing that game. It does kind of haunt you a little bit, because we had a chance to win it all."

When Hold finished his career at South Carolina in 1985, the Arena Football League was just getting started.

As first a player and now a coach, he has been with the league ever since.

"I've been with Arena Football from the beginning, although I didn't plan it that way," Hold said. "It became an obsession with me. Close friends, family, everybody said, 'Why are you doing that? Get a real life, get a real job.' People ask the craziest things, like, 'Do you wear pads?' But I believed in it. It kind of became like a passion to prove that something could happen with it. So I kept doing it, probably against my own better judgment. As it grew, I continued to see the light at the end of the tunnel as to what could happen. It's to the point now where it's not just a job; it's a career."

However, Hold yearns for the day he can return to Columbia.

"I consider Columbia as home," he said. "I can't wait to get back there and go to football games and tailgate."

Chapter 12

TOMMY SUGGS

THE YOUNG LIFE OF TOMMY SUGGS

Tommy Suggs grew up six miles outside of Lamar, South Carolina, working in tobacco as a youngster in the '50s and '60s. He picked it. He cropped it. He lugged it into barns. Until he signed with South Carolina, Suggs had only been to Columbia four times in his life.

"And," he said, "I only lived 50 miles away."

All these years later, Suggs can only shake his head at how his life has turned out. As a quarterback at South Carolina, he is one of a select few who in four years can say he never lost to the Gamecocks' hated rival Clemson. And to think Suggs grew up a Tiger fan, following his family's predilection for orange over garnet and black.

Still, Suggs had plenty of options as to what to do as his senior year at Lamar High School neared an end. A four-sport athlete in high school, Suggs was picked "way down" in the major league draft by the New York Mets as a shortstop.

"I couldn't hit," he said.

That was true not only on the diamond but on the football field. Suggs wanted to play linebacker in high school but that was a no-go.

"I just liked to hit people," he said. "But they wouldn't let me."

Suggs also loved basketball. Up until his senior year, Suggs expected to go to Davidson to play point guard for the legendary "Lefty" Driesell.

While growing up a Tiger fan, Suggs' allegiance changed when Paul Dietzel came on the scene at South Carolina. After winning a national championship at LSU and spending four years at Army, Dietzel left West Point for Columbia to replace Marvin Bass in 1966.

A year later, Dietzel was hot on the trail of Suggs, who was also being recruited by Clemson assistant Art Baker. Baker would later work at South Carolina as an athletic department administrator and consultant.

"I had to call Coach Baker from Paul Dietzel's bedroom at his home," Suggs said. "He had a big recruiting day out there with all these kids in and it was the only place I could find a quiet telephone."

THE SETTING

Freshmen weren't eligible to play football when 5-foot-9 Suggs, who barely weighed 150 pounds, arrived in Columbia in 1967. But the Gamecocks had a freshman team, which went undefeated, including a hard-fought victory over Clemson in a hint of things to come for Suggs.

"It was very intense," Suggs said. "I remember one time we were ahead and Clemson was down to fourth and about a yard and our defensive guys went over to the Clemson coaching staff on the side and pointed at them and said, 'Come on, go for it! Go for it!'"

And the Tigers did. Not only did Clemson not make the first down, but they also fumbled the ball away.

"It just set the tone for the whole Clemson series," he said.

As a sophomore, Suggs left spring practice as the starter. But when he came back in the fall, he had been moved to second team behind Randy Yoakum.

"And we hadn't been on the field yet, which I couldn't understand. I was very disappointed, hurt, mad," Suggs said. "And for the first time in my athletic career—and I go back to the seventh grade and I played four sports in high school—it was the first athletic event I had never started."

While Suggs did come on to replace Yoakum, South Carolina lost that day at home to Duke 14-7. To this day, Suggs says he doesn't know what caused the move to second team.

"No one would ever answer that. I don't know. They just demoted me during the summer," Suggs said. "Randy Yoakum looked like a quarterback. He was 6-2, good guy. We're still friends. We never talked about it. I don't know. I guess I went to the wrong beach or something."

The next week, Suggs came off the bench to engineer a stunning rally against North Carolina, which led 27-3 after three quarters. The Gamecocks scored 29 points in 10:01 to defeat the Tar Heels 32-27 at Chapel Hill.

That spectacular comeback and a 7-3 win over Clemson in Death Valley to end the season were the main highlights of a season in which the Gamecocks finished 4-6. The next year, South Carolina finished 7-4 and won the ACC title with a 6-0 record, capping the season with a 27-13 win over Clemson in what was legendary coach Frank Howard's last game.

But it is a measure of just what the South Carolina-Clemson rivalry means that Suggs didn't pick the UNC game or one of the games along the way that helped the Gamecocks win their only ACC title.

Instead, it was Suggs' final game as a Gamecock, a 38-32 win at Clemson on November 21, 1970, that capped a 4-6-1 season. The win snapped a five-game losing streak that included a 52-34 loss at Georgia and a 20-18 loss at home to nationally ranked Tennessee.

"Preseason, we were ranked 12th or 14th in the country and had a lot of great players," Suggs said. "We didn't have the depth we needed, but we had 25, 27 very good players."

But it was, he added, a "frustrating year."

Not only did the Gamecocks struggle, but Suggs also hurt his ankle—he had always had problems with his ankles dating back to his high school days. He hurt it initially in spring practice and then re-injured it in a 7-7 tie against North Carolina State in Raleigh in the third game of the year.

"I wore a cast for six weeks. They told me I had two choices: stop playing or wear a cast during the week and we'll look at it every weekend," Suggs said. "I decided to wear a cast."

So Suggs wound up wearing a cast all week and having it taken off Friday afternoon. He would then play Saturday and have a new cast put back on his ankle after the game.

"I wore that at practice and I'd take snaps and throw, but I couldn't do anything," he said. "It was my decision and I'm glad I did it."

As the weeks went on and his ankle slowly healed, the cast would come off a day or two earlier in the week, Suggs said. But the real key that allowed him to continue to play with such limited practice was the change in offense.

Until his senior season, Suggs primarily rolled out, getting to the edge, and then having the option of running or throwing. But then Dietzel brought in a new offensive coordinator, John Bridgers, who came from the NFL where he had coached Johnny Unitas and Joe Namath.

"They put me in a drop back, which a lot of people got upset about, but it ended up being my best year ever statistically," he said. "So it ended up being a blessing in disguise because I didn't have to be mobile."

Bridgers would later go on to become the athletic director at Florida State, where he showed a good eye for talent when he hired Bobby Bowden as the Seminoles' head football coach.

THE GAME OF MY LIFE
BY TOMMY SUGGS

As well as I remember, by the time of the Clemson game I was probably off the cast but not at full speed. I was very limited. They brought in special mountain climbing shoes for me. I remember that because mountain climbing shoes had treads but not cleats, so you wouldn't rip your ankle. But you'd have some traction. So they brought those in. I was testing different types of shoes out. But I was very fragile, very fragile.

It was a huge week for me because I grew up a Clemson fan and I was disappointed with the season. A lot of it was injuries. Up there, at that time, there were a lot more pranks going on. You'd drive into Clemson and people would throw buckets of chicken at you. You laugh at it now, but it wasn't funny back then.

Clemson had a pretty good football team, as they always did. But we felt comfortable that if we could stay healthy we could beat them. The game itself was crazy because I think I threw three interceptions in the first half, and I had two individual tackles, I believe, which was amazing.

We were trying to throw quick little slant-ins on them because of some weaknesses we thought they had in their linebacker corps. And it was really, "Don't even look, just three steps, read it one way and throw it," and I did. And twice the linebacker either read me perfectly or misplayed his assignment because he intercepted me twice. I think I ended up tackling him twice.

I went in at halftime. When Coach Dietzel was mad at me, he'd call me "Tom." And so I went in at halftime—I was not happy with my performance. He was standing at the door of the locker room, and he towered over me and said, "Tom, you're eight for eight, three to them and five to us."

That's what he said, which in later years I realized was a fabulous comment. It certainly hit home. In the second half, I came back and threw three touchdown passes. One of the things that was special about it was we were down and came back to win the game.

We had a lot of automatics called that day. One of the automatics we had was when the wide outs read press coverage we had a signal— you'd grab your facemask and I'd acknowledge it back. Jimmy Mitchell, who was one of my best receivers ever, was lined up on my left. We were on the 34-yard line going on.

It was late in the fourth quarter. I looked over at Mitchell and he had press coverage. Mitchell knew he could beat this guy, and I knew he could beat him. So I thought this had "Touchdown" written all over it, and Mitchell was out there, grabbing his facemask, about to shake his helmet off making sure I saw it.

What I was supposed to do was just acknowledge back to him. So I just kind of touched my mask. And he was over there just shaking his head. Then I got under center and tapped the center and he snapped it and I threw the ball 10 yards and he ran 34 for the touchdown. My last touchdown in a regular-season collegiate game was to a good friend, to win the game, beating Clemson; that made it a lot of fun.

Mitchell ended up building my house; we're great friends and we see each other at every football game.

I didn't want that game to end. But afterward, it was just phenomenal, ending my career with a win. I didn't care who I was playing; I just didn't want to end with a loss.

THE AFTERMATH

Suggs would go on to play in the Blue-Gray All-Star game and was named the most valuable player in what would be his last football game ever. He said he had free agent offers from a number of NFL teams.

"Supposedly back then they had some system and Jim Plunkett and I, from what I was told, were about the same in the computer system on about everything until it got to height. Then it just kind of kicked me out," Suggs said.

Suggs said he asked Bridgers, who had been in the NFL, whether he should try his arm at the pros.

"He said, 'Tommy it's like this. You go out there and practice and you throw five touchdown passes and another quarterback 6-5 goes out and throws five interceptions, they cut you because you're 5-9. My recommendation is give it up,'" Suggs said. "And I said, 'Coach, that's the best advice I've ever had.' And I've never looked back."

To this day, however, he is often reminded of what has become his legacy: the last quarterback to go 3-0 (4-0 if you count his freshman team's win) to never lose to the hated Tigers.

"Sometimes I think it's played up too much. I've always told my wife, if I'd have known how important it would have been later in life to win that last game, I'd have been so scared I wouldn't have been able to take the snap," he said.

"It is mind-boggling, and it's sad, because no one has really done that since. It's sad and disappointing. But that's the way it is."

Chapter 13

ROB DeBOER

THE YOUNG LIFE OF ROB DeBOER

Rob DeBoer grew up in America's heartland—and the heart of college baseball to many—in Omaha, Nebraska. While he played baseball and looked like a sure bet to make it to the Major Leagues, DeBoer never had a passion for squatting behind the plate. He'd much rather run someone over in football after having spent hours in the weight room.

"I'll be honest with you, and this is kind of the hidden secret, I never really ever—ever—loved baseball," DeBoer said. "Baseball was never my style. I was into lifting and running and throwing up and lifting some more. And baseball was the opposite. Controlled, not too intense. Repetition, over and over. But I never loved it, not one day in my life."

Growing up, DeBoer was a phenomenal athlete. His father held him back in the seventh grade "purely for athletic purposes," DeBoer said, a trend that was unheard of in the 1980s.

"But it ended up earning me a scholarship," he added. "My junior year I was a good prospect but would never have been a major college football prospect. But my senior year was when everything changed and I was recruited by everybody."

That will happen when you're generously listed as two inches under six feet but turn in a vertical leap in the 36- to 38-inch range and run the 40-yard dash in 4.5 seconds. And, as DeBoer put it, you're a "hard-nosed, north-south guy."

DeBoer was a 10th-round pick in the Major League draft by the New York Mets after his senior season at Burke High School when he hit .613—his career average was .512. He thought about signing with them, but football was his passion.

There was one problem. The schools recruiting him, from nearby Nebraska to Notre Dame to Auburn, didn't want him to play both football and baseball. But South Carolina was willing to let DeBoer do both.

"People don't know this, but I was on a full-ride baseball scholarship, which is unheard of in college baseball," DeBoer said. "So they really recruited me as a baseball player and, 'Oh, by the way, Sparky Woods, we've got this guy who's going to walk on and play football for you.' The rest is history as far as what's next. Then it's all kind of proving time."

But how did South Carolina hear about DeBoer, and what made the Gamecocks think they could steal him away from the Cornhuskers? Jeff Churchich, who played baseball for South Carolina in the mid-1980s, lives in Omaha and had seen DeBoer. He contacted South Carolina assistant coach John Sullivan, who made the trek out to Omaha for a closer look.

"It was unheard of not to go to Nebraska if you grew up in Nebraska," DeBoer said. "I can't explain it. It was just the right fit."

In an odd twist of fate, when DeBoer decided to go to South Carolina, the Cornhuskers signed Cory Schlessinger. "He ends up with three national championship rings and he's still playing in the league [NFL] with Detroit for 12 years," DeBoer said. "It's just kind of interesting how that path changed."

Rob DeBoer. *Photo provided by Collegiate Images/South Carolina*

THE SETTING

While DeBoer was a high-profile baseball prospect, he was a virtual unknown in football around Columbia. He was what DeBoer said coach Sparky Woods and his staff called a "preferred walk-on." And DeBoer wasn't even the highest profile of that ensemble. That honor goes to Cleon Jones Jr., whose father was a member of the Miracle Mets, who beat Baltimore to win the World Series.

While three-year starting running back Harold Green had graduated to the NFL and the Cincinnati Bengals, senior Mike Dingle was back after rushing for 513 yards and six touchdowns.

"He was projected as first-round pick that year. I'm just this little ol' white guy running back from Nebraska that plays baseball," DeBoer said. "But I appreciated Sparky Woods being fair and playing whoever deserved to play. There wasn't anybody that was going to outwork me. So I gradually came to the front of the line and took advantage of the opportunities."

DeBoer will never forget his first game—but only because of what he didn't do. It was otherwise a forgettable debut for DeBoer, who was nowhere to be found in the 1990 football media guide.

In South Carolina's season-opening 21-10 win over Duke, DeBoer was in on three plays. "I missed a block on one. I slipped and fell on the other, and I ran the wrong pass route on the third," he said. "I mean, I was just defeated miserably. I thought, I have no reason to be playing college football. My dad and brother came down. I'm one of those guys that's passionate; I don't want to be just another player. But all of a sudden college football was so big and I was thinking, TV and 80,000 people, and then I screwed up three plays in a row."

So what happened between that and the next week when North Carolina came to town—and the rest of the year, which would see him rush for a freshman school record of 165 yards just over a month later?

"I had a brother and a dad who encouraged me. If I fall, I'm going to get back up, and I had fallen miserably," he said.

And just to show how little his previous outing bothered him, DeBoer said that as he looked ahead to the Tar Heels, all he could think about was that the game was going to be on television and his buddies back home would get to see him play.

All week, he practiced hard on the field and studied his playbook off the field, making sure that if the coach called his number, DeBoer wouldn't make the same mistakes this time around.

With 38 seconds left in the first half, Dingle suffered a concussion and didn't return. And while he was taken to a local hospital, DeBoer began to make a name for himself, rushing for 63 yards on 10 carries, including a 1-yard touchdown, in a 27-5 victory over North Carolina.

THE GAME OF MY LIFE
BY ROB DeBOER

I'm one of those over-prepared people. I panic if my chinstraps aren't buckled. I make sure I've got my mouthpiece. At that time, a lot of people had the mouthpieces that didn't hook onto their helmet. They'd just stick them up on the facemask. I didn't want to be that guy because I didn't want to lose my mouthpiece. So I was more like the walk-on nerds who think they're getting in so they're ready the entire time; my chinstrap was buckled and my mouthpiece was in, even when I was standing on the sideline.

I remember them calling me, putting me in. The first play was okay. I didn't go down easy. The second play was like a 30-yarder; I broke a couple tackles, someone took a blasted shot at me—a big hit—but I broke out of that, slipped another one, and just ran. I caught a pass and broke two or three more tackles. I was so physically exhausted from the hype and the crowd that now I don't even remember them.

When I go back and watch the tape, I remember it was the end of the third quarter. We switched sides on the field and I was thinking okay, I've just run six or seven straight plays. We were down on the goal line and they blew the whistle for the quarter and I had to jog to the other end. And when I watch myself on TV now, I'm thinking, you've got to be kidding me, having to jog all the way to the other end. But I see myself jogging and I remember that back then I thought, 'Am I walking?' because I couldn't fathom having to jog all the way down there.

Then they gave me the carry the very next play. I slipped a tackle, broke a tackle; I was just one of those guys for whatever reason—it's almost strange—I never went down with one guy, almost never. When you look at my highlight reel, and I say this humbly, I had so many multiple-breaking tackle runs that it was strange. I think it's because I was short, with a low center of gravity, and kind of shifty.

I was so physically drained and mentally exhausted I didn't know what to think. It was one of those things where you think, did that really just happen? Did I really have that many good runs? Did I really score my first collegiate touchdown? It was like a dream. I'm one of those guys that give me an inch, I'll take a foot. Give me a little bit of success and man, now I'm really seeing what I can do here. At that point I really started believing in myself, and that if I could do this against North Carolina, I could do this against anybody.

I got thrown into the North Carolina game and I literally broke 10 tackles in one quarter, but nobody knew who I was. I wasn't even in the media guide. But after that, everybody wanted to know who I was. From that point on, it just kind of escalated as I gained confidence. I said to myself, if this first-round draft pick is going to practice and play like that, then I can maybe be a first-round draft pick. So all of a sudden I started thinking that way.

THE AFTERMATH

Dingle returned the next week, rushing for 137 yards and three touchdowns in a 35-24 win over Virginia Tech in Blacksburg, Virginia. But DeBoer burst back into the limelight October 13, 1990, when he rushed for 165 yards and two touchdowns to set the school freshman record in a 37-7 win over East Carolina. Dingle also had a good day, rushing for 113 yards.

DeBoer followed that up by rushing for 104 yards and two TDs a week later in a stunning 38-35 loss to The Citadel. DeBoer finished the season with 700 yards rushing, 46 yards behind Dingle.

Looking back over his dual-sport career, DeBoer said he had one major regret: he wished he had focused on one sport. Had he done that—and football would have been his choice—he can't help but wonder if, like Schlessinger, he might have found a spot in the NFL.

"I don't think I ever played my best college football because I played baseball, too. I think it's impossible," he said.

As a junior, DeBoer was a sixth-round pick of the Toronto Blue Jays and was offered $110,000. But he turned them down because he wanted to play one more year of college football.

The next year he was offered a take-it-or-leave-it deal for $8,000 by the Oakland A's, who picked him in the eighth round. He spent three years in the minor leagues. But he said his focus was on lifting weights, "not hitting, not throwing, not flexibility."

"At that level, that has to be your first priority, but weight lifting was my first priority," he said. "I knew I wasn't going to make it. I hated it. And here's the big secret: I developed that mental block where in every game, I had anxiety attacks about throwing the ball back to the pitcher. I'm telling you it's very real. And I was too proud to get help for it.

"So when you don't love something and you have anxiety about playing every single day, it mentally wears you out. Not too many people know that."

To this day that anxiety remains. When he was asked to throw the first ball out at a South Carolina baseball game, he did so, but not without some anxiety and foreboding as he walked to the mound.

"Everyone asks me, 'Why did you lob it?'" he said. "Honestly, that is a very real syndrome, and I get anxiety every time I have to throw a ball in front of people. But I can go out to my son's Little

League team and throw 100 strikes in a row for batting practice. It's crazy."

Through it all, however, DeBoer looks back with fond memories of his time at South Carolina. Known as one of the hardest working athletes around, DeBoer said he still "never took it as seriously as [he] should have."

"When you're that age you don't realize you can either work now and go on to be a pro athlete, or you can be a great college athlete and it's going to end one day," he said. "I just keep waiting for a 35-and-older, full-contact football league to start up."

Chapter 14

MACKIE PRICKETT

THE YOUNG LIFE OF
MACKIE PRICKETT

Football was ultimately Mackie Prickett's best sport, but growing up in St. Matthews, South Carolina, it was a different sport that provided his introduction to competition.

"My dad was a very competitive person," Prickett said. "We started showing beagle dogs when I was seven. We showed in Atlanta, Greenville, Charlotte—all over the South. And we won a lot."

Then the elder Prickett bought young Mackie a pony.

It wasn't long before the family got into the horse racing business, breeding, training, and racing thoroughbreds in the bush tracks around the state, with Mackie in the irons as jockey.

"I rode horses for four years," he said. "I retired at 13. That's when most of them were starting. But I wasn't the only young person doing that. There were others doing that, too. But I went from there right on into high school sports."

Mackie Prickett was good with beagles and better with horses, but he was at his best with a football under his arm. It wasn't long before the college coaches came calling.

A single wing tailback with speed and moves, Prickett was sought by some of the biggest names in coaching. Coach Paul "Bear" Bryant wanted Prickett to sign with Kentucky badly enough to bring Prickett on a two-week recruiting visit to Lexington.

Near the end of Prickett's visit, Bryant asked him a question.

"He said, 'Son, if you break the line of scrimmage, can you guarantee me you'll score every time?' I said, 'Well, no.' He said, 'Well, I don't want you then.'"

But Bryant did want Prickett. So did almost every football coach in the South in the fall of 1952.

Georgia Tech coach Bobby Dodd traveled to South Carolina to watch Prickett's 11-0 St. Matthews team take on St. Andrews of Charleston for the Lower State championship. Prickett admits the game wasn't exactly a shining moment for him or the team.

"The first play from scrimmage, I broke off a 65-yard run, but one of their players stripped the ball from me and ran the other way for a touchdown," Prickett said. "They kicked off, we fumbled, and they ran it in for another touchdown. They kicked off again, and on the first play from scrimmage, the center snapped the ball over my head, and they picked it up and scored again. One minute into the game, we were down 20-0. They went on to beat us something like 42-20."

After the game, Dodd approached Prickett: "He said, 'Nice game, son.'"

And Georgia Tech did offer a scholarship, but Prickett decided he wanted to stay closer to home. That meant South Carolina or Clemson. The elder Prickett made the choice for his son.

"Daddy loved all people," Mackie said. "He sold insurance for a living and made his living with people. But he didn't like anything about Clemson. Nothing. And he couldn't stand Coach [Frank] Howard. He came to our back door once, and Daddy just said, 'No, no.'"

So, almost by default, University of South Carolina coach Rex Enright got a player who would turn out to be one of the best he ever had.

Mackie Prickett. *Photo provided by Collegiate Images/South Carolina*

THE SETTING

When Mackie Prickett arrived at the University of South Carolina in the fall of 1953, he had two big surprises waiting for him.

The first involved academics. He had carefully studied the various curriculums at South Carolina and chosen pharmacy because it didn't require history, a subject he hated.

"Wouldn't you know it," Prickett said. "The very first course was the history of pharmacy."

By the time he got to the football field, he was in for another surprise; the coaches wanted to move him from tailback to quarterback.

Prickett says his year at quarterback on the freshman team was a struggle: "I had a horrible time. The first two games were a nightmare. Then coach Weems Baskin, who coached the freshmen, called me in and told me how horrible I was and that they were moving me back to halfback. It took two weeks to move back up the charts. I was at my natural position and I played well. Coach Baskin actually apologized. But in the spring, they wanted me back at quarterback."

Prickett struggled along at quarterback in the spring but gradually began to show improvement. His improvement continued into the fall, and by the week of the 1954 season opener against 18th-ranked Army, he was on the second team at safety and quarterback with a reasonable expectation of playing.

But what happened next exceeded all of Prickett's expectations.

THE GAME OF MY LIFE
BY MACKIE PRICKETT

You wouldn't have thought I'd get the chance to play against Army if you had seen me early in the spring. I was running about fourth or fifth team. Playing quarterback just wasn't natural to me. Then a player got hurt, and Coach Enright said, "So help me God, you can't be as horrible as you have looked. So go back in and take the second unit."

I went back in with what I think was one of the best backfields at South Carolina and we were on the second unit. We had Ed Adams at fullback, a transfer from Cornell. He was a monster. He was 225 pounds and could run over you or outrun you. Ed was such a monster that we just whipped the tar out of the first unit. We also had Bill Tarrer, and Tommy Woodlee, an Atlantic Coast Conference sprint champion.

We went to play Army and we were big underdogs. They were ranked No. 1 in the East. We went in there and got behind 14-0, and Army was marching down the field on us. Coach Enright stuck the second unit in to see if we could stop them, and I was lucky enough to get an interception on about the 5-yard line.

We advanced back down the field on them and we got to midfield and had fourth and two. Instead of punting like we should have, I ran the option and broke loose for about five or six yards and a first down, with Coach Enright on the sideline choking on a glass of water. We got down to about the 20, and I threw a pass to Mike Caskey and he took it in for the touchdown. I don't remember how things went exactly after that, but we kept on pouring it on. It was a lot of our blending good running and not much passing. I think I had one long run and a couple more key runs, and we wound up winning 35-20.

That was a breakout game for me. I had other good games. I think I scored two touchdowns later that year when we beat Clemson. My senior year, we beat Duke for the first time in 30 years. But the Army game got my career started. It was a breakthrough; you've got to have a breakthrough in anything.

THE AFTERMATH

South Carolina's stunning victory over 18th-ranked Army on the opening weekend of the 1954 college football season was one of the biggest upsets of the year.

The Gamecocks came into Army's Michie Stadium as 14-point underdogs and were given very little chance at the upset. Equally improbable was the performance of Prickett, who had struggled so much learning the quarterback position.

However, South Carolina finished the game with a whopping 446 yards rushing, racked up 21 first downs and only punted twice. Prickett led scoring drives of 96 and 80 yards. The 96-yard drive started after Prickett intercepted a pass while playing safety.

Prickett said he never did get nervous about playing in front of a hostile crowd in Michie Stadium in the first game of his college career.

"Practice was so hard, playing in the game was an absolute pleasure," he said.

South Carolina didn't follow up very well after its stunning upset. The next week, West Virginia trounced the Gamecocks 26-6 in Columbia, and one play in particular sticks out in Prickett's mind: "The first time I ran the option, Sam Huff ran over me," Prickett said.

"The coaches wanted to know what [had] happened. I said, 'I don't know.' But he didn't tackle me the rest of the game; I was on the lookout for him. They beat us pretty bad. I guess we celebrated that Army win too much and let it go to our heads. And that Huff boy, ugh."

South Carolina went on to finish 6-4 in Prickett's first season at quarterback.

The Gamecocks slipped to 3-6 in 1955 but rebounded in Prickett's senior year to finish 7-3, thanks to a couple of promising young running backs just up from the freshman team—Alex Hawkins and King Dixon.

The final game of Mackie Prickett's football career came in the Blue-Gray College All-Star game. As luck would have it, Bear Bryant, then coaching at Texas A&M, coached the Gray, and he had not forgotten Prickett.

"He gave me a hard time all week," Prickett said.

Also playing in that game were future Kansas City Chiefs quarterback Len Dawson, future Los Angeles Rams star Jack Pardee, and future college football television analyst Lee Corso.

"I saw Lee Corso a few years ago, and got a chance to visit with him," Prickett said. "He told me I was the worst passing quarterback he'd ever seen."

When Prickett's college career was over, he turned to the sport he'd known as a child—horse racing.

In partnership with his father, who handled the breeding and breaking of young horses on the family farm in St. Matthews, Prickett began a career as a trainer.

"I took nine horses down to the Holly Hill (South Carolina) Training Center, where Lucien Lauren would eventually bring Secretariat," Prickett said. "That's how I got started."

For 10 years, Prickett and his wife, Jackie, raced horses primarily on the New England circuit, racing at Suffolk Downs, Rockingham, and the now-defunct Narragansett Park. The Pricketts finally decided they wanted a more stable environment to raise their young family, so they returned to their hometown of St. Matthews.

Mackie tried to stay in the horse racing business as a breeder, but found it to be a struggle.

"I would raise 20 to 25 horses a year and put them out on deals with people," he said. "I was supposed to get 25 percent of the earnings. But it's hard to collect from people."

Mackie Prickett put his degree to use and began a career as a pharmacist. He and Jackie raised three sons—Dalton, Keever, and Phillip—all of whom became doctors. Mackie and Jackie Prickett celebrated their 50th wedding anniversary on November 24, 2006.

"I lost my father our third year at the track, and it was like I lost my right arm," Mackie said. "He took care of the home base, breeding and breaking and getting them ready to come to me. When Daddy died, it was an uphill struggle from there. It was hard to spend nine months away from home.

"The luckiest thing we ever did was stop racing. It enabled the kids to establish themselves. Of all our accomplishments, those children are what we're most proud of."

Chapter 15

BRAD EDWARDS

THE YOUNG LIFE OF BRAD EDWARDS

Brad Edwards grew up in a family where sports were important, and where baseball was the most important sport of all.

Brad's father Wayne played college baseball at North Carolina State as well as professionally in the minor leagues, and Brad's older brother Jeff also excelled at the sport, going on to become a scout for the Colorado Rockies.

Thus, it was only natural that Brad Edwards' first exposure to competition came on the baseball field.

"They took me out when I was six or seven years old to get started playing coaches' pitch baseball," Brad recalls. "They put me at third base. Then, they didn't have the skunk rule where they stop the game if it gets out of hand. The other team comes up to bat, and they're hitting the ball and just coming around the bases and coming around the bases, scoring run after run. I'm just standing there, getting mad. I was a really competitive kid. Finally, I started kicking sand at them as they rounded third. Then I started pushing them, and then I finally tackled one. I was escorted off the field. The next day, my parents told me that I was no longer on the team and informed me, 'You're in the wrong sport, kid. You should be playing football.'"

Actually, that was not the end of Edwards' baseball career. He was a two-sport star at Douglas Byrd High School in Fayetteville, North Carolina, as a pitcher in baseball with a blazing fastball, and as a highly touted quarterback in football.

The scholarship offers came pouring in for both sports, but Edwards had his heart set on playing college football.

When he visited Florida State, Edwards thought he had found his college home. However, he began to have second thoughts the moment he announced to his family that he planned to play quarterback for coach Bobby Bowden's Seminoles.

"My mom started crying when I walked in and announced I was going to FSU," Edwards said. "It was so far away."

That was just the beginning of Edwards' second-guessing.

He was standing in the hall at Douglas Byrd High School one day, just after announcing his decision to attend Florida State, when assistant football coach Curtis Frye walked by.

"I hear you're going to FSU," Frye told Edwards. "You'll be a good college quarterback, but I think you can go to the pros as a safety."

It was as if Frye had turned on a light bulb over Edwards' head.

"Coach Frye just said that and walked off, leaving me standing there stunned," Edwards said. "Well, you tell a 17-year-old kid that, he's likely to believe you. The more I thought about it, the more I thought I'd really like to play safety."

Edwards was convinced, but the colleges recruiting him were not.

Florida State's coaches told Edwards he would never see the field as a defensive back for the Seminoles, who were absolutely loaded in the secondary and had just received a commitment from a young corner named Deion Sanders.

Edwards then called South Carolina assistant coach Tom Gadd and told him he'd sign with the Gamecocks under the condition he would be allowed to play safety.

Brad Edwards. *Photo provided by Collegiate Images/South Carolina*

"There was a stunned silence on the phone," Edwards remembers. "Finally, he said, 'OK, whatever you want to play, we'll take you.'"

And that's how Edwards discovered the position that would ultimately propel him to a nine-year NFL career.

Frye's words would prove to be prophetic. Years later, Frye, now the head track coach at the University of South Carolina, still jokes about it with Edwards.

"He tells me he made me a lot of money with his advice," Edwards laughs. "I think what might have been at quarterback and what John Elway and guys like that were making, and I tell him that he actually may have cost me a lot of money."

THE SETTING

Brad Edwards' transition from high school quarterback to college safety wasn't exactly seamless.

The sum of Edwards' experience in the secondary amounted to a few games in the high school playoffs while filling in at safety for an injured teammate.

"The first day we got to South Carolina for preseason practice, all the secondary guys took off running," he said. "Our whole practice on the defensive end was sprinting. It was all conditioning. Meanwhile, the quarterbacks were just dropping back and throwing. I was like, 'What have I gotten myself into?' I was really concerned about my decision. But I stuck with it and kind of committed myself to being good and getting in good shape and that kind of thing."

There were other things to learn.

"I had no idea how to play," Edwards said. "The secondary coach pulled one of the other players aside and said, 'Can you take Edwards on the side and teach him how to hit people?' I really had no idea."

By the 1984 season opener against The Citadel, Edwards had improved, but not enough to expect significant playing time.

With barely a minute left in the game and South Carolina clinging to a 31-24 lead after a late touchdown, special teams coach Jim Washburn screamed for Edwards.

"Go in on the kickoff team," Washburn told Edwards. "You're the contain guy. We're kicking to the southeast corner."

A bewildered Edwards ran onto the field only vaguely aware of his assignment.

"I had never really covered kicks," Edwards said. "I didn't have a clue that other teams will sometimes put two or three men on the contain guy. All of a sudden a guy from The Citadel ear holes me out of nowhere. Their return guy is running free down the sideline, and I'm thinking, 'My career is over.'"

Fortunately for Edwards, the Gamecocks' Chris Major hauled down Bulldogs return man Mike Lewis at the 23-yard line.

South Carolina's Otis Morris intercepted a pass with nine seconds to play to seal it for the Gamecocks.

"Walking off the field, I just felt terrible," Edwards said. "It was like, 'You idiot freshman.' So that's how I got started."

Edwards was feeling better about his situation after the Gamecocks started 9-0, and eventually finished 10-2, recording the most victories in school history.

And by his senior year in 1987, Edwards had long made up for his rookie mistakes and was one of the cornerstones of a talented defense that was combining with a potent offense to produce another of the Gamecocks' best teams ever.

The Gamecocks rolled to a 7-2 start and a No. 12 ranking in the AP poll, with a 13-6 loss at Georgia and a 30-21 loss at Nebraska serving as the only blemishes on their record heading into a November 21 showdown at home with archrival Clemson.

The Tigers were 9-1 and ranked ninth, and the game was to be played before a national television (ESPN) audience.

THE GAME OF MY LIFE
BY BRAD EDWARDS

For me, this game was the most memorable because I knew it was going to be the last home game of my college career. I thought maybe I would get a shot to at least try out somewhere in the NFL after it was all over, but again, I couldn't help thinking about it being my last time playing in Williams-Brice Stadium. That's more of what I remember—just soaking in that whole week.

I remember driving around in a car with our quarterback, Todd Ellis, and Clemson quarterback Rodney Williams the Tuesday night before the game. If our fans knew we were riding around together, or even talking to each other, they would have killed us. But we did a lot of stuff with their players. Rodney and I went back to being at quarterback camps together in high school. Our fans had no idea we had that kind of camaraderie. I couldn't have imagined us having an on-the-field brawl, as was the case in 2004. There was just not that kind of animosity between the athletes. But when the lights went on and we stepped between the lines, it was like, "I'm going to take your head off."

I remember the bus ride over, just looking at everyone. And being in the hotel. And just every step of that week. More than anything, that's what I remember—the week before that game.

It was a night game on ESPN, and when we got to the stadium, it was already getting cold. I think the temperature was in the 40s, which is cold for South Carolina. Sometime in the fourth quarter, we were leading 13-6 and they had the ball coming out at about their 40-yard line. Joe Lee Dunn, the defensive coordinator, called a blitz. Well, if you're bringing seven people, the tight end has no choice but to block and so does the fullback. So I know they're going to get a two-man pass route if they run play-action in the passing game. Sure enough, that's what they run. I know if the quarterback looks outside to the receiver, he's going to do one of two things—he's coming in or he's coming out. It's that simple. I just got into position, and as soon as the quarterback looked, I knew it was going to be the out route. I broke on the ball and picked it off and ended up scoring a touchdown, putting us ahead 20-7. That really cemented that game for us. It was odd, because I had picked off a pass the year before against Clemson and run it in for a touchdown. After the game, the locker room was just crazy.

The next week, we lost at Miami 20-16, and they went on to win the national championship. And then we got shellacked 30-13 by LSU in the Gator Bowl. We were so stinking close to being a really good team. We should have been a 10-win team that year. But that Clemson win was special. Nobody had to explain to me how important the Clemson game was, and is. If you're going to play well in one game, it better be that one. I knew that already, but I had no idea to what degree. Even now, all these years later, people will come up to me and say, I remember that play you made in the Clemson game in 1987.

THE AFTERMATH

Brad Edwards' 40-yard interception return for a touchdown with 5:47 remaining indeed put the clincher on South Carolina's 20-7 victory.

Clemson's only score of the game came on the Tigers' opening drive, when they marched 91 yards, with Wesley McFadden scoring on a two-yard run to put the Tigers ahead 7-0.

Field goals of 49 and 45 yards by South Carolina's Collin Mackie cut Clemson's lead to 7-6, and the Gamecocks took a 13-7 lead on a six-yard touchdown run by Harold Green.

South Carolina's defense held the Tigers to 166 yards in total offense, the lowest ever for a Danny Ford-coached Clemson team.

The Gamecocks would lose to Miami the following week in the last game of the regular season and then lost to LSU in the Gator Bowl to finish 8-4, with a ranking of 15th in the final AP poll.

Clemson went on to beat Penn State in the Citrus Bowl to wind up 9-2. The Tigers finished the season ranked 12th.

Making his final appearance in Williams-Brice Stadium was a big reason why the 1987 game with Clemson provided Brad Edwards with one of his fondest memories as a football player at South Carolina.

Edwards found himself in a familiar setting in 2005, when he accepted a job as Director of New Business for Action Sports Media, a company that sells advertising space at stadiums and arenas.

Edwards' office is located in Williams-Brice Stadium in a room that once served as the meeting room for the secondary.

"I like to say that I have really gone nowhere in my life, because my office is back in my old meeting room," Edwards jokes.

Actually, Edwards has seen and done quite a bit since his college football days. He was drafted in the second round of the 1988 NFL draft by the Minnesota Vikings and got a quick education in the business side of pro football.

"I had a two-year deal there with an option bonus," Edwards recalls. "At the end of it, The Vikings said, 'We're not going to renew your contract.' The next day, they called and said, 'Ok, we're ready to get you signed.' When I asked about my option bonus, they said, 'Technically, we're not liable for that.' That was my first taste of big city business. So that's how you save $100,000. I said, 'Nah, if you guys want to pay me the money, fine. If not, I'll just go on.' The next day (Washington Redskins coach) Joe Gibbs called me. Fortune smiled."

Edwards spent seven years with the Redskins, made it to two Super Bowls, and was rewarded with a ring in 1992 when Washington beat the Buffalo Bills 37-24 for the title. He had two interceptions in the game.

"I had a pretty good career, both at South Carolina and in the pros," Edwards said. "I feel blessed to have earned a Super Bowl ring. I know this: I'm not giving it back."

Chapter 16

J.D. FULLER JR.

THE YOUNG LIFE OF J.D. FULLER

J.D. Fuller grew up at the tail end of Jim Crow in the small, rural South Carolina town of Cross Hill, a textile and farming community where some whites still harbored the remnants of racism.

"I never saw a lynching," Fuller said matter-of-factly. "But my grandfathers would tell me about things. I felt I kind of lived it through them. I was going to go to the University of Auburn, and my daddy told me not to go any further south.

"He said, 'No, son, we're far south enough. I worked in Alabama as a boy and I was mistreated, and I don't want you to go to Alabama.'"

Both his grandfathers had, in earlier times, sharecropped. They later moved on to work in timber and the mobile home industries—for a man in the Cross Hill community who was a known racist.

One day, Fuller stopped at the man's store to sell some empty drink bottles, a widely practiced form of entrepreneurship by youngsters in the south looking to make a little money.

"Put the bottles here," the man said.

"Huh?" Fuller replied.

"Huh? You don't 'huh' me," the man replied. "I'll break this bottle on your head."

Fuller would have none of that.

"I was probably eight or nine. I remember bracing to say, 'You won't hit me with the bottle. I'm not going to let you hit me with the bottle.' I can't remember exactly what I said, but I remember communicating to him, I'm not going to let you hit me with the bottle."

In telling his family and friends the story later, they looked agog at the young J.D., shocked that he had stood up for himself. "I guess [the store owner] thought I should say, 'sir,' but I was a customer. Even then I knew I was a customer," he said.

Ironically, the man was a huge Clemson fan, which didn't help the Tigers when they recruited Fuller—in basketball and football.

Not every white man was a racist in Cross Hill. During his days at Clinton High School, Fuller worked for a man who, every Saturday morning, would come pick up Fuller, waiting outside the teenager's home in the early morning hours until he woke.

"He wouldn't even blow his horn. I always felt like he knew I played a game Friday night, probably partied a little bit," Fuller said. "Then I would go to his house and he'd fix me breakfast and we'd sit there and eat and talk. I would do probably an hour of work. He'd pay me for three. So for every one that was awful, there was one of these guys."

Growing up, Fuller played football and basketball—he was the MVP of his team as a sophomore—and ran track. He also played catcher in the sandlots, the same position his father played for the Cross Hill Black Sox.

Early on, basketball was Fuller's sport. In fact, he and his brother, Rufus, tied in a one-on-one tournament at the Bell Street Junior High. "We went into like three overtimes and then the coach finally just called it a tie," Fuller said. "Looking back, I'm kind of glad he did."

Fuller didn't play basketball as a senior, concentrating on football and listening closely to his cousin, Calvin Hill, who was now with the Washington Redskins after a stellar career with the Dallas Cowboys, where he was named the NFL's Rookie of the Year.

J.D. Fuller Jr. *Photo provided by Collegiate Images/South Carolina*

"I used to go up and visit him at the Redskins' camp," Fuller recalled. "We'd run, lift weights, play basketball. He was a big influence both athletically and academically because he went to Yale. He'd tell me how important education was over sports."

Fuller was recruited by a host of schools. But on the day he was to sign with Georgia, he got a visit from South Carolina coach Jim Carlen, who made a last-ditch pitch. While Fuller was an All-America middle guard, he wanted to play linebacker in college—and Carlen knew it.

"He said, 'Listen, you can play any position on my field,'" Fuller said. Then came the clincher: "He said, 'Georgia needs you. But I've got to have you. Look, Georgia's got fabulous players in their own state. Let them get their own players,'" Fuller recalled.

That appeal sold Fuller on the Gamecocks.

THE SETTING

Fuller played enough as a freshman in 1979 to letter while being credited with 10 tackles, which was only a hint of hits to come. Fuller would have more than 100 tackles in his last three seasons and finish his career with a school-record 405 stops.

Then Fuller earned the starting middle linebacker job as a sophomore—no doubt in part because his chief competitor for the job had forgotten his notebook one day, which cost him "a demerit." But on the first play of the year, Fuller dislocated his elbow.

"My elbow bone was sitting up here on my tricep," he said.

Fuller was given a medical red-shirt, which he initially didn't like but later came to see the merit in. As a sophomore in 1981, Fuller was in on an incredible 143 tackles on a team that lost its last three games to Pacific, Clemson, and Hawaii, to finish the season 6-6.

"I was making a lot of tackles. But it seemed like I was chasing a lot of people," he said. "So the stats might have been a little bit inflated because people were running off leaving us."

At year's end, Carlen was fired and was replaced by assistant Richard Bell, who had coached Fuller and the other linebackers.

While Fuller continued to play well, coming up with 121 tackles, the Gamecocks struggled to a 4-7 record that included a stunning loss to Furman.

South Carolina's final win was a 17-14 victory over Navy in the penultimate game of the season. On paper that game could easily be overlooked—especially in light of the 56-26 pounding Florida State put on South Carolina one week earlier in Columbia—except for one thing.

Fuller made what may have been—no one is sure—a school-record 22 tackles, 12 solo and 10 assists against a Navy team led by running back Napoleon McCallum, who would go on to be a two-time All-American and set 26 school records—including being the school's all-time leading rusher.

THE GAME OF MY LIFE
BY J.D. FULLER

I remember it was kind of a big relief because we had lost a lot of games leading up to that one. I remember just talking to Coach Bell about what I could do to get us ready. I remember him saying just line up and play. It all came together in Navy. We controlled the game. I had a lot of tackles.

They had a guy, Napoleon McCallum. I ended up stopping him several times, and not just me. Some other guys had good games, too. I just remember we never let him get off the line and we kind of restricted him throughout the game.

One of the things I remember most is the football calendar for the next year; there's a picture of me tackling Napoleon. In the photo, I am right under him. It was kind of a perfect tackle: lock-up, take him to the ground. Probably over half of my tackles happened with him right there on the line of scrimmage.

I just remember feeling good the whole game. I had come to the conclusion we were not going to have a great season. But we were trying to finish that season on a positive note. I felt like the coaches had confidence, too, and that they were digging in to try to finish strong and get ready for next year.

We had some good players. That Furman loss took a lot out of everybody. Of course, rumors started flying about Bell's future, so that was distracting. But the Navy game got us into a zone and saying, "Hey, listen, I'm going to go out here and knock some people down today and make some tackles and help my team win and do whatever it takes."

It was like I was in a zone the whole game, just running around making hits all day and knocking people down. Napoleon didn't say a lot. I think I did most of the talking, saying things like, "Not today. Not today." But it was a good clean game. Not a lot of trash talking. But it was a great feeling: smack, hit him right at the line of scrimmage, lock him up, take him down. I don't think I missed a tackle.

It seemed like I was in the right place all day long.

THE AFTERMATH

After a season-ending 24-6 loss at Clemson, Bell was gone, replaced by former New York Giants running back Joe Morrison, the "man in black" who came to town in cowboy boots and with a quiet demeanor.

Fuller was moved to outside linebacker. He pulled a hamstring during spring practice that continued to bother him all the way through his senior season. But the injury wasn't enough to stop him from making 131 tackles.

With another disappointing season over—South Carolina finished 5-6—and Fuller's college career over, he pondered his future. The Washington Federals picked him in the USFL draft in December and offered him a $3,000 signing bonus and a $26,000 salary. But Fuller decided to return for his final semester to earn his degree.

Fuller later received a $9,000 signing bonus from the New York Giants. But after two preseason games, he was cut. While "nobody's really knocking the door down," Fuller did have feelers from teams in the USFL and CFL. But he decided it was time to move on. He wasn't getting any younger, and the bumps and bruises and injuries had slowed him—and the rest of his life was beckoning.

"After graduation, I decided I was going to give [the pros] one go. If it worked out, fine. If it didn't, I'd do something else," he said. "There's all these stories about guys that kept trying and ended up not getting their careers started. They're 30, 35 and just getting started in the real world."

But he wasn't done with South Carolina. While running his own employment agency, someone pointed out that his alma mater had listed him as "one of the all-time leading tacklers" in school history. As part of his advertisements for his business, Fuller used that information, saying he was the school's all-time leading tackler.

"I was very concerned that somebody would say, 'You're a liar,'" he said. "Of course that hurts your business and everything else. So I really kind of took it personal at that point."

So he contacted the school. Officials told him he was right and that they would correct the mistake. But Fuller waited and they never did.

"I was pissed off," Fuller said. "I'm the one that sacrificed my body."

So he wrote athletic director Mike McGee, whom he said responded "very, very slowly." So he wrote University president Andrew Sorensen. That, Fuller said, "is when I started getting a response."

Eventually the records were corrected.

As he looks back on his time at South Carolina, Fuller knows had he chosen to go to Georgia or Clemson he would have a national championship ring—both the Bulldogs and Tigers won titles while Fuller played for the Gamecocks.

"But that's not quite as important to me now," he said. "I was the first one in my [immediate] family to graduate. I have other siblings that graduated also. I felt like I was a good influence on them," he said.

His cousin, Calvin Hill, kept on him about school as well: "[Hill] used to always tell me about athletes who never finished school and never went back. They put too much into the whole sports thing.

"I remember even in my high school and hometown folks would kind of give you, 'Yeah, you're a good athlete but surely you're not smart enough to go to college and finish college.' I just remember that was part of my motivation; it probably had a lot to do with Calvin. I wanted to prove I could do more than just play football. I didn't want to be a dumb jock."

Chapter 17

WILLIE SCOTT

THE YOUNG LIFE OF WILLIE SCOTT

Willie Scott Jr., the oldest of three children, was born on Friday the 13th into a family that valued education. His parents were both educators, and his mother, Gloria, was one of the first African-Americans to teach at Newberry High School in the late 1960s after integration.

His grandparents put five sons through college, and his grandmother, Daisy Abrams, never asked her 6-foot-5, 245-pound grandson about his football exploits, which included being arguably the greatest tight end ever at the University of South Carolina and a first-round NFL draft pick.

But so concerned was she that he graduate with the rest of his class that Scott took 24 hours—15 or 16 being the norm—during the second semester of his senior year, a time when most future NFL players are skipping classes.

"She never asked me if I was going to go to the pros," Scott said. "She asked me if I was going to graduate on time. All I could say was, 'Yes, ma'am.'"

His mother taught math, his father coached and was an assistant principal and, later on, principal. His aunt was also in education. His sister, Pamela Scott-Johnson, went on to get her Ph.D. in psychology and neuroscience from Princeton University and is now chairperson of the Department of Psychology at Morgan State.

But the Scotts were also an athletic family. The elder Scott played football and basketball at Claflin College in Orangeburg, South Carolina, and his sister played basketball and ran track.

Young Willie Scott also learned how to play the piano and trombone, but it was obvious he was a talented athlete. When he was 12 he said he won the state "pitch, hit, and throw" contest, earning his family a trip to an Atlanta Braves game against the Cincinnati Reds.

"We got to sit in the dugout and did our thing between innings. I got to meet Hank Aaron and Frank Robinson and Johnny Bench and Joe Morgan, the whole 'Big Red Machine' crowd," Scott said.

"After that, we sat in the stands and it began to rain. So we left, and Hank Aaron hit two home runs after we left."

Scott seemed to play every sport at Newberry High School, earning a dozen letters, including one in tennis his freshman year. But the next year he moved to track—he did the high jump, long jump, and triple jump, while also running the anchor on the 440-yard relay—and never returned to tennis.

He also played baseball—he was a first baseman—and basketball. While some schools recruited him in basketball, Scott decided the sport held only limited long-term prospects.

"I knew I wasn't going to get any taller than 6-5," he said. "So I decided I better stick with this football thing."

Scott was pursued by a number of schools, including Clemson, which had former Tiger tight end Bennie Cunningham, who was now with the Pittsburgh Steelers, call Scott.

"I was thinking about Clemson, I really was," Scott said. But he just felt South Carolina was the place for him, and it didn't hurt that one of his father's fraternity brothers was Harold White, a one-time assistant football coach and longtime athletic department administrator at South Carolina.

Willie Scott. *Photo provided by Collegiate Images/South Carolina*

THE SETTING

Upon arriving in Columbia in 1977, Scott was assigned No. 47, an odd number for a tight end and far from the No. 84 he wore in high school. But coach Jim Carlen assigned numbers based on position, with kickers and quarterbacks wearing 10-19, defensive backs 20-29, and so on.

"It was a weird number," Scott said, "but that's what they gave me when I came in. It was one of the few that was left."

While the Gamecocks struggled to a 5-7 record, Scott saw more and more playing time as the season went on, finishing with nine catches for 132 yards. As a sophomore Scott had 13 receptions—four for touchdowns—for 127 yards. But South Carolina again struggled, finishing 5-5-1.

Along the way, however, Scott got some advice he not only took to heart but still remembers to this day from Ken Shipp, who had been offensive coordinator with the Houston Oilers. Shipp was friends with Carlen and helped him out as an unofficial coach, working with Scott, among others.

"He told me something when I was a sophomore. He said, 'Willie, I've been watching you. You can run pretty good. You can catch pretty good. If you work on this weight lifting thing and get that body to get through a 20-game (NFL) season, you'll be a first-round draft pick,'" Scott said.

"I was like, 'Yeah, okay,' or 'Whatever.' But I kept working."

As 1979 rolled around, optimism was high for the Gamecocks, who opened the season with a 28-0 loss at North Carolina in a game that featured four players who would go on to be first-round NFL draft choices in 1981, including future Heisman Trophy winner George Rogers of South Carolina and Tar Heel linebacker Lawrence Taylor, who were the first two players drafted.

"Coach Carlen brought us in and said, 'Okay, you've been reading your own press clippings,'" Scott said.

The Gamecocks then won five straight before losing again, falling 18-17 at Notre Dame on October 27. "I got sick that week," Scott said, adding he was put into the school infirmary from Wednesday to Friday. "It was awful. I didn't tell my momma I was in the hospital until I was out."

South Carolina would win three of their last four regular-season games, losing only at Florida State 27-7 while beating Clemson 13-9 in the rivals' regular-season finale. But the season ended with a disappointing 24-14 loss to Missouri in the Hall of Fame bowl.

Still, South Carolina had finished 8-4 and, Scott said, there was a feeling "it was all coming together'" heading into 1979, especially after Rogers had rushed for 1,681 yards.

The Gamecocks opened the season by outscoring their first two foes 111-0. But the next week South Carolina lost at Southern Cal

23-13. Among those playing for the Trojans was Chip Banks, who was from Augusta, Georgia. Scott had served as Banks' host for his official recruiting visit to South Carolina.

"I saw in the paper where he didn't remember who took him out on his visit," Scott said. "I had a pretty good game against him. Oh, you don't remember me, huh? Okay, take that."

The following week the Gamecocks headed to Ann Arbor to take on Michigan and coach Bo Schembechler, who didn't talk to Carlen before the game.

"Coach Carlen was the nicest guy, but [we'd heard] they wanted the visiting team to come out and then they wanted to come running out [into the Gamecocks]. If they do that, we're going to start a fight," Scott said. "We're all kind of looking around like, 'Did Coach Carlen say that?' It was like, 'They don't think we can play football. Let's show them what we can do.'"

And South Carolina did, stunning the Wolverines 17-14.

The Gamecocks would again finish the regular season 8-3, earning a spot in the Gator Bowl against Pittsburgh. Both teams were ranked—South Carolina was 17th and the Panthers were No. 4 and hoping to capture the national championship under coach Jackie Sherrill.

The game featured more than a dozen players who would go on to play in the NFL, including Rogers, fresh off winning the Heisman Trophy, and Pittsburgh's Hugh Green, who finished second in the Heisman voting and won the Outland Trophy.

While Scott's 109 yards would set a school record for receiving yards, which was broken in 2005, the Gamecocks fell 37-9. But given all that surrounded the game—and the fact it was Scott's last college game and the abundance of talent on the field—it is the game Scott will always remember.

THE GAME OF MY LIFE
BY WILLIE SCOTT

This was a highly touted game. George had won the Heisman. Hugh Green was second. People were figuring we're already stopped because not only did the other team have Hugh Green on one side, they had Rickey Jackson on the other side. So everybody thought we were beat.

We were going out to eat for a team function. Pittsburgh was there before us. I saw Hugh Green coming out. I'd never met him before. Coach Larry New, the defensive line coach, said, "Well, Willie, that's Hugh Green. He doesn't even know who you are, son. Where's Newberry, South Carolina?" That was his whole demeanor, how he did his defensive players, too, saying, "He's going to kick your tail all over the field."

I went off on him. I said, "You don't worry about Hugh! I'll take care of him! Where's Natchez, Mississippi? I don't know where it is! You don't worry about Hugh! I'll take care of Hugh." Coach Carlen pulled me aside and said, "Now Willie, you know not to get into anything with Larry."

Sometimes I was against Hugh and sometimes I was against Ricky Jackson. It was a tough battle. He won some. I won some, caught a few passes out there. It was a real tough game.

We had a pretty decent first half. I got the ball on a delay route right before the first half, got down to the 1- or 2-yard line but we didn't score. Time ran out. It just deflated us.

They were still in the hunt for the national championship. So they had to beat us pretty badly. I had a few blocks in the game. I think Hugh was negated to maybe five stops that whole game. That record I got in that game was just broken recently by Sidney Rice. So it's lasted 25 years. That's not too shabby.

I counted up one time and there were 14 people in that game who went to the pros, and seven of those were first-round draft picks. That's just from Pittsburgh. So they had to beat us pretty good.

Things went slowly in that game. We just couldn't get over the hump. We turned the ball over. I don't know what could have happened if we had gotten into the end zone at the end of the first half. What was the score, 17-3? If we'd scored, it would have been 17-10. But we weren't too far out of it. But they came back and beat us up pretty good in the second half.

It's always tough losing your last game. You can listen to any coach, any player—they hate losing the last game. But in retrospect, the things that we did at the university in 1979 and 1980 were significant; we were the first team to go 8-3 back-to-back seasons in the history of the school. Then we had two guys drafted in the first round and got a Heisman Trophy. That has yet to be repeated at the university.

THE AFTERMATH

His college career over, Scott turned his attention not to the NFL but to making sure he graduated on time—for himself, his family, but most of all, for his grandmother.

Scott said basketball coach Frank McGuire asked him to join the team after football season was over. But he declined, saying he couldn't possibly do that and take his 24-hour class load.

"I told him I've got to graduate," Scott said. "My grandmother's going to kill me if I don't."

But still there was the NFL draft. Scott was projected as a first-round pick. The projections were correct. Scott was the 14th player picked, and the only tight end to go in the first round—to the Kansas City Chiefs.

Scott heard he was a first-round pick by chance. He was back in his dorm room between classes when the Chiefs called. The team wanted him to fly to Kansas City right then.

"I told them I wasn't sure I could make it. Tuesday was my long day of classes," Scott said. "Finally I did the O.J. Simpson thing, running through the airport. I missed my first flight."

Less than 24 hours later, however, he was back in Columbia to give a motivational speech at a local school as part of a class project. Scott also missed the first few days of mini camp, which happened to fall on the weekend he was scheduled to graduate.

"I told them I could come on Monday," Scott said. "But I've got graduation on Saturday, and I've got people coming to see me graduate."

Scott spent eight years in the NFL, five with the Chiefs and his final three with the New England Patriots, finishing with 89 receptions for 766 yards and 15 touchdowns. Scott said he would love to have had two more years in the NFL, but he was released after the 1988 season and decided it was time to get on with the rest of his life.

Scott said he had a good career at South Carolina, saying he and the rest of his teammates took pride in helping Rogers win the Heisman Trophy while also winning 16 games their final two seasons.

"It's history," he said, "and we're all a part of it."

What Scott would like to be part of is the coaching staff at South Carolina; it's no secret that Scott has long dreamed of being an assistant coach for the Gamecocks.

He was a graduate assistant under Sparky Woods, and he interviewed twice with coach Lou Holtz. And he sought an interview with coach Steve Spurrier before his first season as well as after it.

"People don't want to talk about it, but we've had people come back and be a coach in every other sport except football. Football has never had a full-time former player come back and be a full-time assistant," he said. "Think about that. It's frustrating."

Chapter 18

KEVIN LONG

THE YOUNG LIFE OF KEVIN LONG

Kevin Long says he has a running back's heart in a lineman's body. He knew early on that running the football was what he was meant to do. It just took the rest of the world a bit longer to figure it out.

Long remembers going out for football in the eighth grade at now-defunct Bell Street High School in Clinton, South Carolina.

"When I went out for the team, I didn't know how to put pads in the pants or anything," Long said. "I was totally green. I always had this notion that I wanted to be a running back, but the coach had other ideas. I was a tall, lanky kid, but I wasn't that big. I was probably about 170, about 6-1. You just didn't see any tall running backs back then."

Since running back is a popular position, Long's coach had a special play to discourage those he felt weren't suited to playing it.

"They had this play called T99," Long remembers. "What they would do was put all the upperclassmen on defense. They'd just hand you the ball and tell you to run straight up the middle. The first time I tried to play running back, they handed me the ball and I ran up the middle. They literally held me up; they gang tackled me, and a guy broke my nose. That's how brutal it was. I went over and sat on the fence. An assistant coach came over and gave me a bucket of water. He said, 'When you get finished cleaning your nose up, come over here with us linemen.' So I basically played offensive line."

With the advent of integration, Long moved over to Clinton High School, but he was still penciled in as a lineman.

"I still wanted to play running back," he said. "I was the fastest guy on the team, and here I was on the line. But the coach kept saying no."

Long turned his back on football during his junior year and focused his attention on track and field.

"I ran track and did everything—high jump, sprints, field events—and I ended up being the most valuable player in track," he said. "Later on, the high jumping would prove very beneficial to me as a short-yardage back because I was a good leaper. You get to third and one… that really paid off for me later in the pros."

His exploits in track made the football coach sit up and take notice.

"After my junior year, the coach said, 'OK, I'll give you a shot at running back,'" Long said. "They put in the wishbone and I was a fullback in the wishbone. But the way they ran it was kind of like the way the Cleveland Browns used to run it. Sometimes you're in a pro set, sometimes you're in the wishbone. To make a long story short, we ended up winning the state championship that year and I was the most valuable player on the team. So my senior year was the only year I played running back in high school."

College scouts weren't exactly knocking down Long's door. He had an offer from hometown school Presbyterian College, in those days an NAIA school. South Carolina State offered a partial scholarship, but Long couldn't afford less than a full.

It appeared he had the answer to his problems when the Naval Academy offered him an appointment.

"I actually signed a letter of intent to go to Navy," Long said. "But we didn't have a car and I had to be at Shaw Air Force Base in Sumter to take a physical on a Thursday morning at 6 a.m. I couldn't get any of my relatives to take a day off from work to take me down

Kevin Long. *Photo provided by Collegiate Images/South Carolina*

there. I kept waiting for the people from Navy to call me back, but they never did."

Late in the recruiting season, the University of South Carolina became interested in Long.

One day, Long was at his after-school job, driving a forklift at a mobile home manufacturing plant, when South Carolina assistant coach Dick Weldon wheeled his car right into the yard and right in front of Long's forklift, forcing him to a stop.

Long got down off his forklift to hear what Weldon had to say.

"Coach Weldon got out of his car and we talked for a few minutes," Long said. "He said, 'We really want you at South Carolina.' Then he put the letter on the hood of the car and I signed it."

THE SETTING

Long just assumed that he had signed with the Gamecocks as a running back, but he was in for a surprise when he arrived on campus.

"I went there thinking I was going to play running back," he said. "The night after the first team meeting, they said, 'Everybody go see your locker.' I went over to the running back section and looked and looked and there was no locker for Long in the running back section. So I went over to the linebacker section, and there's No. 58, Kevin Long."

Once again, coaches had sized up Long's powerful physique and figured he would be better suited to another position.

But Long was adamant about playing running back, and his tenure at linebacker proved to be short-lived.

"I lasted about a week at linebacker," he said. "I just couldn't handle playing it. I just didn't have the desire to be a linebacker. I said, 'Coach, I'm a running back. I don't want to play linebacker.' Back then you didn't just tell a coach what you wanted to do. He said, 'Well, if you want to play running back, you have to play on the practice squad.' So I went down there. Clarence Williams and I were running backs on the practice squad. We spent most of our freshman year running the other team's plays against the first-team defense. That was 1973. Back then, freshmen couldn't play on the varsity anyway. But it probably worked out the best for me because it gave me an opportunity to hone my skills at running back since I had only played one year."

Long found himself a backup running back during his sophomore year, but with the Gamecocks off to an 0-5 start, coach Paul Dietzel decided to give Long a shot.

Long rushed for more than 100 yards in four of South Carolina's final five games, and the Gamecocks finished 4-7. That still was not enough to save Dietzel's job.

South Carolina hired Jim Carlen, and once again, Long had to prove himself worthy to another coach.

The Gamecocks began the season with a senior player as the starting tailback.

"We were playing Georgia Tech in the season opener, and I was on the bench watching the game," Long said. "Coach Carlen came down there and said, 'Son, why aren't you in the game? I want him in the game and he's not to come out until I tell him to come out.' I had a good game, and we ended up winning and the rest is history."

Long would soon prove to be a cornerstone in one of the most prolific offenses in school history.

The Gamecocks were 5-2 in 1975 when they headed to Raleigh, North Carolina, to take on Lou Holtz-coached North Carolina State.

THE GAME OF MY LIFE
BY KEVIN LONG

We went up to their stadium, and I remember the day was really humid and it seemed like the fans were right on top of us. We were both pretty good teams. We were 5-2, they were 5-3, and both of us were fighting for a bowl game.

North Carolina State had some really good players. They had a great running back named Ted Brown, who went on to play in the

NFL, and they had the Buckey twins, Don and Dave, who played wide receiver and quarterback. It figured to be an offensive game, and it was. It just went back and forth. We were just running up and down the field on them, just ripping off yardage in 15-, 20-, and 30-yard clips. But they were doing a pretty good job of keeping us out of the end zone. They just had one of those kinds of teams.

We drove 80 yards and took the lead for good with a little over a minute to play on a touchdown run by Clarence. We had to go for two, but we got it, and it looked like we were going to win the game 21-20. But they drove down the field on us and scored with nine seconds to play to win the game. I finished that game with 160 yards on 27 carries, which was the most carries I'd ever had in a single game and the most yards I'd ever had in a single game. I think Clarence had a bunch of yards rushing, and I'm pretty sure we had over 500 yards in total offense.

It was one of those games where we were totally exhausted once it was over. On paper, we should have won that game. It's hard even now to accept that we lost. But from a runner's standpoint, it was one of the most satisfying games—breaking tackles, scoring touchdowns. All the elements of that game made for a memorable matchup. It was a fantastic game with a crazy finish. We did everything but win.

THE AFTERMATH

North Carolina State's 28-21 victory over the Gamecocks was indeed a thriller.

The Wolfpack drove 65 yards in the last 1:29, with Timmy Johnson scoring the game-winning touchdown on a 1-yard run with nine seconds to play.

The two teams combined for 909 yards in total offense, and the miraculous thing for the Gamecocks was that they managed to score only 21 points.

South Carolina's veer offense piled up 407 yards in total offense, 378 of which came from the running game, with Long supplying

160 of those yards. Williams rushed for 120, and quarterback Jeff Grantz added 57 yards.

The Gamecocks led 10-0, only to see the Wolfpack rally to take a 20-13 lead.

Then South Carolina drove 80 yards, with Williams scoring on a 5-yard run with 1:29 to play. The Gamecocks went for two, with Grantz passing to tight end Brian Nemeth for the conversion, putting them ahead 21-20.

It took the Wolfpack six plays and 1:20 to answer with what proved to be the game-winning touchdown.

South Carolina would go on to finish the season 7-4 and earn a bid to the Tangerine Bowl in Orlando, Florida.

Long and Williams each rushed for 1,000 yards on the season.

After finishing his career at South Carolina, Long was drafted in the seventh round of the NFL draft by the New York Jets.

The Jets had just hired Walt Michaels as head coach to replace Lou Holtz, who was fired after one very unsuccessful season.

Unlike Long's high school and college teams, the Jets had no preconceived notions that Long should play a position other than running back. He spent five years with the Jets. His best year was 1978, when he rushed for 954 yards and 10 touchdowns.

The Jets eventually traded Long to the Chicago Bears, who had just hired Mike Ditka as head coach. Long had a training camp run-in with Ditka, who was less than enamored with Long's request for a day off when his wife had the couple's second child.

"They released me on the last day of camp, and it was the happiest day of my life," Long said. "I thought it was over."

Not quite.

A call from coach George Allen persuaded Long to give the fledgling USFL a shot, which he did. But when the league folded, Long's career was over.

He tried several different professions after football: working for a bank, then selling insurance, and then real estate. He finally settled on his present career, driving a truck and delivering vending machine products to merchants in North Carolina.

Long still follows the Gamecocks and has fond memories of his time at the school and his career as a running back, even though so many people initially thought he was unsuited for the position.

"Sometimes you just know, you have that gut feeling, that burning desire down in your heart," he said. "Everybody else says you can't, a little voice says you can. I don't know why, but I always felt I was a running back."

Chapter 19

RICK SANFORD

THE YOUNG LIFE OF RICK SANFORD

When Rick Sanford was growing up in Rock Hill, South Carolina, in the 1960s, his older brother Steve always made sure to include Rick in pickup football games in the neighborhood. Rick thought it was nice of his brother to let him participate in games with the older guys.

Years later, Steve confessed to a different reason.

"Steve told me, 'Did you ever think there was a reason why we let you play with us in the field? You were seven and eight years old out there playing in that field with 15- and 16-year-olds and they couldn't catch you,'" Rick said. "That was the reason they let me play. It wasn't because they really liked me or anything. Steve said I was as good as the rest of them when I was seven and eight."

Rick Sanford excelled in football, basketball, and baseball as a youngster. He added track and field to the mix in high school. He was a natural. Sanford was bigger, faster, stronger and more skilled than nearly every kid in town.

"Looking back on it now, I do think I was blessed to do a lot of the things that I could do," Sanford said, "but I worked at it, too, through the years.

"That was one thing about growing up in Rock Hill. We had great youth sports. The one thing I can say is that I was blessed growing up with the YMCA and the youth programs we had. If you were athletic in any way, you could develop it."

By the time he was a senior at Northwestern High School, Sanford had a decision to make. He was being heavily recruited by schools all over the country in both football and basketball.

"I actually had more basketball offers than football," Sanford said. "The ones I was serious about in basketball were Wake Forest and Oklahoma. Oklahoma had a guy named Alvin Adams who went on to play for the Phoenix Suns. But ultimately, I didn't want to go as far away from home as Oklahoma. In football, Clemson did a great job of recruiting me, but Clemson, especially back then, was so isolated. There just wasn't a lot to do. Plus, I had grown up a Carolina fan. It came down to basketball at Wake or football at Carolina."

South Carolina was undergoing a coaching change in 1975. Paul Dietzel was out and Jim Carlen was in.

Carlen knew he had a potential star in Sanford, and he knew that Sanford also was seriously considering basketball.

"I think what swayed me toward football was Coach Carlen," Sanford said. "He told me, 'There are a lot of 6-2 guards playing in the NBA, but there aren't a lot of 6-2 defensive backs who can run like you can and can hit like you can playing in the NFL.' I thought, 'He's got a point.'"

THE SETTING

Sanford wasn't an immediate starter for the Gamecocks as a freshman in 1975, but he got plenty of playing time, mostly in nickel back situations.

"That was the thing about Coach Carlen," Sanford said. "He was very loyal to the older players. You needed to be a lot better than the player ahead of you if you were going to start as a freshman. I

Rick Sanford. *Photo provided by Collegiate Images/South Carolina*

admired that about him, and I got some valuable experience my freshman year."

Sanford and the rest of the South Carolina defense was not the story in 1975.

The Gamecocks of 1975 had one of the most prolific offenses in school history, with two thousand-yard rushers in the backfield in Clarence Williams and Kevin Long, and one of the most gifted dual-threat quarterbacks in the country in senior Jeff Grantz.

South Carolina finished 7-5 in 1975, and while the Gamecocks went to the Tangerine Bowl that year, they lost to Miami of Ohio 20-7.

The highlight for the Gamecocks instead was a 56-20 thrashing of Clemson.

Sanford recorded his career interception, picking off a Steve Fuller pass on the final play of the game.

With most of the talent on offense about to graduate, and a bunch of young, talented faces on defense, South Carolina's emphasis was about to shift, and Sanford would eventually find his way into the spotlight.

In 1976, the Gamecocks were 4-2 heading into a showdown at home against 4-2 and 20th-ranked Ole Miss.

THE GAME OF MY LIFE
BY RICK SANFORD

We had some really good games with Ole Miss while I was at South Carolina. The year before, down in Oxford, Mississippi, we got into a real shootout with them. Jeff Grantz won it for us with a late touchdown pass.

This game was different. It was a defensive struggle all the way. It was a very physical game. A low-scoring game like that, there's a lot of defense. I just remember waking up the next day and feeling so beat up and injured. I felt like I had been in a 15-round boxing match after playing these guys. They were a really physical team.

They had this running back named Reg Woullard, a hard runner, but shifty. It was late in the game and it was 10-7 and we were ahead. They had driven the ball downfield on us and had got to the 10-yard line with about a minute left to play. I was playing left cornerback. They were running the option and flipped it back to Woullard. I was standing at the goal line and went up to meet him, and when I hit him, the ball flew out. I just saw the ball physically fly out. I think I got my helmet on it. Bill Currier fell on it in the back of the end zone for a touchback and we won 10-7. We could have easily lost, not necessarily because of the play at the end. With his momentum, he would have scored if didn't lose the football and they would have won the game.

The other thing I remember about the game is that I actually injured my knee on that play. I missed the Notre Dame game the next week because of it. I regret that, because we really had them on the ropes and could have won that football game.

I think I gained a lot of confidence from the Ole Miss game at that point of my life. I felt like I kept getting better after that. In spring ball before my senior year, my secondary coach, Dale Evans, came to me and told me he had been talking to the pro scouts and all the combines had me rated as the top defensive back in the country. I was shocked. I had no idea. I just thought I was a pretty good football player.

THE AFTERMATH

South Carolina's game with Ole Miss on October 16, 1976 was truly an old-fashioned defensive struggle, and there's no doubt the play Sanford and Currier made at the end of the game saved it for the Gamecocks.

Ole Miss ran the ball 43 times for 56 yards rushing, but did manage 163 yards passing.

South Carolina would finish with 273 yards in total offense.

The Gamecocks got on the board first with a 19-yard field goal by Britt Parrish in the first quarter, but Ole Miss would take a 7-3 lead into the half after a 10-yard touchdown pass from Tim Ellis to Curtis Weathers late in the second quarter.

In the second half, the game really settled into a defensive struggle.

South Carolina finally got a break after a shanked punt by the Rebels set up the Gamecocks at the Ole Miss 29-yard line.

Four plays later, South Carolina scored what proved to be the only points of the second half on an eight-yard touchdown pass from quarterback Ron Bass to tailback Clarence Williams with 5:45 to play in the third quarter.

That gave South Carolina a 10-7 lead, but it would be up to Sanford and Courier to save the day.

Late in the game, Ole Miss drove to the South Carolina 10-yard line where the Rebels faced second and five.

The Rebels pitched it to Woullard, who appeared headed for a touchdown until Sanford met him head-on at the goal line and forced the fumble that Currier would recover in the end zone.

The victory elevated the Gamecocks to 5-2. However, the victory over Ole Miss would prove to be the high-water mark. South Carolina proceeded to drop three of its last four games to finish 6-5.

Sanford became the first player in school history chosen in the first round of the NFL draft when the New England Patriots selected him with the 25th pick of the 1979 draft.

He would go on to play six years with the Patriots and one with the Seattle Seahawks, mostly at safety. But it was while playing pro football that Sanford stumbled upon a different career track.

"I was having a sciatic nerve problem, back problems, my second year in pro football and I was getting no help from any of the treatment," Sanford said. "I finally went to a chiropractor and he was the one who saved my career. After that I thought, 'Well if he can do that for me, I'd like to do that for other people.' Before that, I had thought I might go into coaching or into scouting. That's where I was headed, but I decided this was kind of neat. Seventeen years later, here I am.'"

Dr. Rick Sanford operates a chiropractic clinic in Irmo, South Carolina, and of course still follows the Gamecocks.

"I look back on my career and I think it didn't matter where I would have played," Sanford said. "I'm glad I came to Carolina, but I think I would have made it anywhere.

"I'll always follow the Gamecocks. They will always be near and dear to my heart, although sometimes they hurt my soul."

Chapter 20

BRYANT GILLIARD

THE YOUNG LIFE OF BRYANT GILLIARD

The second of five children, Bryant Gilliard grew up in the small southern town of Hinesville, Georgia, less than an hour south of Savannah. He dreamt of playing not college football—that was assumed, he says—but of someday displaying his talents in the National Football League.

"I come from a town that produces athletes yearly," he said. "It's amazing. In fact, two of the guys a little older than me—Spencer Clark and Al Stevens—went to Carolina before me. So I grew up watching those guys excel in sports."

Gilliard, who from childhood had the nickname "Mookie," lettered in four sports at Bradwell Institute, which was founded in 1871 by Samuel Dowse Bradwell. Bradwell was a captain of the Liberty Volunteers and was badly wounded in the Battle of Atlanta, but he managed to return home to Hinesville. For years it was a private school, but later it became a public high school.

Had integration not taken place when he was a youngster, Gilliard would not have wound up at Bradwell, which was closer to his home. He instead would have had to go to the all-black high school on the other end of the county.

While Hinesville is in the Deep South and was devastated by the Civil War, Gilliard said he doesn't remember any major racial problems growing up.

"There wasn't necessarily a black section or a white section," he said. "Even to this day, it's just families all over the place, not just one area is considered the black part of town."

Gilliard is convinced athletics played a part in that, saying many in the community united to cheer on the local sports teams regardless of race; sports were a uniting force.

From eighth grade on, Gilliard was convinced he was destined to play college football, which was a big reason why, while in eighth grade, he moved from running back to wide receiver.

"I just thought that would present another opportunity for myself," he said, "and I wasn't crazy about getting hit."

As a sophomore, he was one of the starting receivers for Bradwell but was also working with the defensive backs; the starting free safety moved after his father, who was in the military, was transferred. Gilliard ultimately was moved to free safety full time, although he did see limited action at receiver.

"My junior year, the first game of the season, we were down and they put me in for a two-point conversion," he said. "They actually threw a pass to me, and I caught it. That was probably the last time I played offense."

By the end of his junior year, Gilliard was hearing from colleges interested in signing him up for a scholarship. The letters multiplied during his senior season, which saw Bradwell finish 10-0 but lose in the first round of the playoffs 1-0. Under the rules, if a game ended in a tie in the playoffs, the teams would play two five-minute overtimes. Then if both teams had still not scored, the winner was decided by total yardage.

His high school career over, Gilliard looked ahead toward college. But he made only two visits—to nearby Georgia Tech and to South Carolina. He made the trips along with his high school teammate and lifelong friend Dominque Blasingame. Both signed with the Gamecocks, although Gilliard said it wasn't planned that way.

Bryant Gilliard. *Photo provided by Collegiate Images/South Carolina*

"We didn't have a pact," he said. "It's strange. We never really asked each other about where one or the other was going to go and we ended up there together."

THE SETTING

The Gamecocks were coming off an 8-4 season in 1979 and would have another 8-4 campaign in 1980, with Gilliard contributing as a true freshman. Gilliard recovered a fumble by Wake Forest on a kickoff return in the fourth quarter that led to a touchdown and a 39-38 win for South Carolina on November 15.

But in 1981, Gilliard didn't play. Coach Jim Carlen and his staff decided to red-shirt him, which didn't sit well with Gilliard.

"It was tough because guys, Dominique in particular, came in and weren't red-shirted," Gilliard said. "And when you are an athlete who was 'the man' from whatever high school you went to, the last thing you want is not to be able to play.

"I have to say I was no different. I felt I should be out there. I didn't realize the bigger picture. It actually worked in my favor."

After the Gamecocks finished 6-6 in 1981, Carlen was gone, replaced for just a single season by Richard Bell, under whom South Carolina would struggle to a 4-7 record. Gilliard said he wasn't all that concerned about who was the head coach.

"I was just looking for an opportunity to play," he said.

But his year ended early when he tore his left knee's anterior cruciate ligament in the middle of the season. Not only was he sidelined for the rest of the year, but he missed the Gamecocks' first spring practice under new coach Joe Morrison.

Still, he came into the fall as the starter, which Gilliard said was a result of his hard work during the off-season. Along with running and lifting weights, Gilliard also was checking up on Morrison.

"I wanted to find out more about him, what type of program he had prior to coming here," he said. "So I read up on him. I felt him coming in was definitely going to be a benefit not only for me, but also for the school."

Gilliard was right, although it would take a year for that to happen for the Gamecocks, who finished 5-6 in 1983. The year was highlighted, however, by a stunning 38-14 victory over Southern California on October 1 at Williams-Brice Stadium.

"That was just unbelievable," Gilliard said. "I probably slept two hours the whole night after it. I couldn't wait to get up. I think I got up about 5:30 and went and got a newspaper. It was in print. It actually happened."

As 1984 rolled around, Gilliard said he and his teammates felt something special might be in the offing. Gilliard was elected by his teammates as a co-captain of what would turn out to be the best team in school history.

It was the year of "Black Magic"—with apologies to Johnny Cash, Morrison was South Carolina's "man in black"—and "Fire Ants," the Gamecocks' swarming mass of defenders.

Before two-a-days, the players all got haircuts. Some shaved their heads entirely. Others went for the Mohawk look. Gilliard imitated the look of the television star "Mr. T."

"We all became nuts," he said. "My girlfriend could not believe it. She was to the point of tears because she never thought I would do that."

The year started with a 31-24 win over The Citadel. And after a 21-0 victory over Duke, the Gamecocks held off Georgia 17-10, a win that Gilliard said had the players saying, "Hey, we've got some potential here."

Three weeks later, South Carolina went to South Bend, Indiana, and held off Notre Dame 36-32. "You go in there and you want to win," Gilliard said, "but sometimes you doubt yourself and, thinking of all the prestige that Notre Dame has, it can be overwhelming."

After victories over East Carolina and North Carolina State in Raleigh, North Carolina, the Gamecocks were 8-0 and ranked No. 5 in the nation—the school's highest ranking ever to that point—as they prepared for their final home game of the year against No. 11 Florida State, which was 6-1-1 and had, two weeks earlier, manhandled defending national champion Miami.

The Seminoles led the nation in scoring at 38.6 points—South Carolina was seventh at 34.5—and had only one interception and nine turnovers overall. But South Carolina would force seven turnovers—including four interceptions alone by Gilliard—to beat FSU 38-26 in a game televised nationally by ABC.

Among those on the FSU sideline was graduate assistant Brad Scott, who a decade later would become South Carolina's head coach and lead the Gamecocks to their first-ever bowl win.

But that November afternoon belonged to the Gamecocks and Gilliard.

THE GAME OF MY LIFE
BY BRYANT GILLIARD

I can't say there was anything really different about the week leading up to the game. I don't think I've ever had an anxious game. Of course, I read biblical scriptures before games; that is where I seek comfort. But what it also does for me, and continues to do for me, is relax me. It relaxes me to the point that prior to a game, someone usually has to wake me up. I sleep the entire time. I never really worry about television. Just leave me alone. I have peace and quiet. I'm fine.

Even as I was growing up, I was the same way. I remember before one of my games—I had to be in maybe the eighth grade—I fell asleep and the coach had to come to my house. Fortunately I only lived a mile and a half from the field. But the coach had to come wake me up because I was able to relax in that situation.

It started out as any normal game day: we went out for the pregame stuff. Then, like in all games, we came out to the theme song from *2001: A Space Odyssey*. That was just enough to get the blood really flowing. Inside, I'm just ready to go, just ready to get it started, to get this first hit in and get the juices really going.

We got out on the field, and next thing I knew I made one interception, but I was unable to advance it. At that time, my goal had been to get one interception per game. The next thing I knew, I ended up with a second interception and then a third one. I think I actually caught that one in the end zone.

With that third interception, I started thinking, I'm not going to just down it; I'm going to try to actually run it. I saw what I thought was an opening. As I headed out of the end zone, I got plowed by one of their receivers. He had come out of nowhere—I didn't see him. I guess he was hidden by one of my teammates, and boy, did he lay a shot on me. My whole right arm went numb. But I held onto the ball and got up. I'd been thinking, I'm going to take it 100 yards. I didn't. I got really popped on that one.

Once I made the third interception, I realized they were getting desperate. They needed to score quickly. So in order to try to think like them—meaning that I knew they had to go up top—I took a deeper drop to make sure no one got by me, and if they did get behind one of the corners, I would still be able to help. So I was probably playing about 15 yards deep as opposed to playing the norm of about nine or 10 yards deep. Doing so helped me see the ball better.

The fourth one: I think I actually caught that one in the end zone, too. That was probably my favorite one. I really had to go up and out-jump the receiver. It was kind of a two-man battle. If I missed it, he caught a touchdown. So we both jumped up. We both grabbed onto the ball. As we came down, the ball somehow came alive—neither one of us had a hold of it. But as I hit the ground, it popped into my hand.

I don't know who the photographer was, but I still have a picture of me and Hassan Jones going up for that one, like a jump ball; I have two-thirds of the ball and he has about a third, and he's behind me. It's a great picture.

We were up 24-7, but we didn't seem able to stop them the way we wanted to, especially when we needed to, going into the fourth quarter. We thought, "We need to hold onto this and make sure we get a win out of this whole thing." And then we really started to hunker down and play good defense in the end.

There were still some critics who didn't think we were as good as we were, that we just caught a team on a bad night or something along those lines. I was hoping that victory would silence some of those doubting Thomases for us.

I think I was asked if I had ever had a game like that before. While in high school, I actually did have a game that, at the time, I thought I would never surpass. I think in that game I had two interceptions, one returned for a touchdown, and I had a punt returned for a touchdown. But to now have a game where I had four interceptions—that was incredible.

THE AFTERMATH

For his performance, Gilliard was named the national defensive player of the week by *Sports Illustrated*, which sent him a plaque that he still has—at his mother's house.

"That was unbelievable," Gilliard said. "Talk about dreams, I can't say that was even a dream. I was glad to get that one. I was big smiles once I actually read it in the magazine."

But the smiles soon faded for Gilliard and the Gamecocks, who climbed to No. 2 nationally behind Nebraska, which remains the highest ranking in school history. The Cornhuskers lost the next week to Oklahoma—but so, too, did South Carolina, falling to Navy 38-21 in Annapolis on November 12 in an upset that is seen by many as the single-worst loss in school history.

"That day—now you talk about a day being different. For me, I didn't feel right that day. No matter what I did, I didn't feel right," Gilliard said. "I remember it was pretty cold. I actually brought my thermal with me.

"After we went for pregame, I came back in and put my thermal back on because it just did not feel right at all. I figured maybe if I'm able to warm myself up I'll feel a lot better, feel like I'm really into the game. It just never happened at all. That day, the entire day, just did not feel right."

South Carolina beat Clemson 22-21 the following week but ended its season with a 21-14 loss to Oklahoma in the Gator Bowl, a far cry from the Orange Bowl, which the Gamecocks looked like a sure bet for had they beaten Navy.

Gilliard's college career was over—and all too soon, so was his dream of playing in the NFL. Gilliard went undrafted, which surprised him. He signed a free-agent contract with Tampa Bay but didn't make it past the first cut.

"I definitely thought I would make the NFL," he said.

With that, Gilliard decided to get on with the rest of his life. Within about a year he began working for Federal Express and today is a senior manager in New Jersey for the company.

"I said, 'Let me get on with my life.' People said maybe I should have tried out again. I'm not one who wants to accept a handout from anyone. This is a decision that I made. Now I need to go on and move on with my life and get a real job," Gilliard said.

"It was tough. I'm not going to say that it wasn't. It was very tough to actually get to the point of getting past that because for years growing up, that's all I've done; I've played sports. I've always been one of the better athletes at whatever sport it was that I was playing. Now I no longer am.

"It's an adjustment period. I can tell you there were days that I would just sit for hours trying to figure out, why? What happened? I'm supposed to not be here sitting at home with nothing to do, having to look for a job. The course of your life changes completely."

And as he joined the "real world," Gilliard reflected on the lessons he learned from Morrison and his assistants.

"Those guys, oh, man, they challenged us like you wouldn't even believe," Gilliard said. "They really taught the importance of preparation and hard work. If you do that every day no matter what you're doing, you're going to be successful...you can't lose. You're guaranteed to win."

Chapter 21

PHIL PETTY

THE YOUNG LIFE OF PHIL PETTY

Phil Petty, who grew up with two older sisters and was a lifelong Gamecock fan, played football almost as soon as he could walk. And soon enough, he was running. The five-year-old Petty didn't play quarterback; he was a running back.

"I was always pretty much the fastest kid on the field," Petty said. "But I could also throw."

And so in the eighth grade his arm got him moved to quarterback, and he was home. "They [wanted me] to play quarterback. So I gave it a shot," he said, "and I loved it."

Along with football, Petty was a shortstop and pitcher in baseball and a shooting guard in basketball. He quit playing baseball when he got to Boiling Springs High School but continued to play basketball as well as football until his senior year, when he focused solely on football.

"I'd already committed to South Carolina and didn't want to risk injury," Petty said.

Petty earned the starting job at Boiling Springs midway through his sophomore season and credited coach Mac Bryan with giving him the confidence to believe he could play major college football.

"He probably had the biggest impact on my life as far as coaches at a young age," Petty said. "He timed me in the 40-yard dash and saw me throw the spring before my sophomore year. He said, 'If you do what I tell you to do, you can write your ticket to college.'

"I remember I was young and those were probably the most exciting words I had ever heard. Him saying that was definitely a motivating factor for me. ...Ends up he was right."

Petty said the highlight of his high school career came during his senior year in the first round of playoffs, when he threw four touchdown passes in a game against defending state 4-A champions Walterboro, giving Boiling Springs a 42-40 lead.

It was the first playoff game ever held at Boiling Springs—and it was the Bulldogs' first playoff victory in a decade.

As a quarterback Petty was a BMOC—Big Man on Campus—a title that he didn't particularly like either in high school or later at South Carolina.

"I was kind of uncomfortable with it at first because I was kind of a shy person and a very humble person," he said. "I did not like the attention. That was the biggest adjustment, but that helped prepare me for playing in Columbia."

Petty always assumed he'd wind up playing for his beloved Gamecocks, but that didn't keep him from making official recruiting visits to Tennessee, North Carolina, and Clemson, as well as South Carolina.

The letters poured in from recruiters.

"You get to the point where you separate the bulk mailing from handwritten letters," he said, "and you just read the handwritten ones. That was the way I did it anyway."

As he headed to Columbia, Petty knew he would be making a number change to emulate his hero, Notre Dame and NFL star Joe Montana, after wearing no. 9 at Boiling Springs.

"I was going to be either 14 or 16 in college, that was for sure," Petty said. "Montana was my hero, my idol."

THE SETTING

Petty was red shirted as a freshman in 1997. While Petty didn't play, coach Brad Scott allowed him to travel with the Gamecocks

Phil Petty. *Photo provided by Collegiate Images/South Carolina*

when they played Georgia in Athens, Mississippi State in Starkville, Arkansas in Little Rock, and Tennessee in Knoxville.

"He wanted me to see the arenas in the Southeastern Conference to see what I was going to be playing in," Petty said. "I remember we were playing at Georgia. He said, 'Take a good look around. This will be you next time we're here.'

"It kind of gives you chills. [Playing there] does take an adjustment, especially when you're playing in those arenas of 80,000 and 90,000 people plus. It's not something you do every day."

There was a moment during the year when Petty almost had his red shirt yanked off. Petty said Scott considered the move when starter Anthony Wright was hurt against Tennessee with two games left.

After losing to Tennessee 22-7, the Gamecocks were 5-4 and needed a victory over Florida or Clemson to go to a bowl. Ultimately, Scott decided to go with Vic Penn for Wright and keep the red shirt on Petty.

The Gamecocks lost their last two games.

"That was kind of a pivotal point in our season," Petty said, adding he was "very grateful in the end" that Scott made the decision he did.

As 1998 rolled around, Petty knew Wright was the starter. Petty just hoped to see some playing time, which he did. But the season was a nightmare. The Gamecocks beat Ball State 38-20 to open the season but then lost the next 10 games, which led to Scott's firing and the hiring of legendary Lou Holtz.

With rumors swirling that Holtz was coming out of retirement (and the broadcast booth), Petty said he and the players had the same reaction as many fans: "He's not coming to South Carolina."

"But lo and behold it happened. It definitely blew our minds."

Petty will never forget his first meeting with the diminutive Holtz.

"We were all in awe of him," Petty said. "First of all I remember thinking, 'Wow, he's not a real big man.' But...he's probably the most intimidating person I've ever met."

That judgment would not change when practice rolled around that spring. While known as a hard taskmaster with his players, Holtz is particularly hard on quarterbacks, who must withstand his withering onslaught or forget about any chance of playing.

"He's very demanding," Petty said. "That was quite an adjustment." One that Petty wasn't sure he was willing to make; he considered transferring.

"You think, maybe I need to go somewhere else. Maybe this isn't the right place for me," Petty said. "I wasn't sure of him. He wasn't sure of me. There were a lot of closed-door discussions."

The year itself was memorable only for its misery. The Gamecocks lost more than a dozen offensive linemen to injuries and failed to win a game under Holtz, going 0-11 to extend their losing streak to 21 straight games. The season started with a 10-0 loss at North Carolina State in a monsoon and ended with a 28-19 loss at archrival Clemson.

Four games in, Petty hurt his knee and missed five games, coming back to play in a 33-13 loss at Florida and then the Clemson loss. The day after the season-ending loss to the Tigers, Petty got a call in his dorm room from Holtz.

"He said, 'We're going to protect you. We're going to build this thing. Just hold tight,'" Petty said. "I think that was his way of saying he believed in me, and my way of saying I believed in him and the University of South Carolina, and I was obviously staying."

After 21 straight losses, no one would have predicted the Gamecocks were poised for the best two-year run in school history. South Carolina would finish 8-4 in 2000 and 9-3 in 2001, finishing each season with victories over Ohio State in the Outback Bowl, making Petty the only quarterback in school history who can boast of two bowl wins on his résumé.

To put that in perspective, the Gamecocks have won just three bowls total in more than a century of football.

While some might scoff, Petty said he knew South Carolina was close to turning it around. The nearly two years of losses, he said, made them "tough, mentally and physically."

"It made us hungry and determined," he said. "We were kind of like a dog backed into a corner, and not just with other teams criticizing us but even our own people at times. There were a lot of people questioning, 'Can South Carolina get it done? Can Phil Petty get it done?'"

The answer was yes. Along the way, the Gamecocks also answered another question: Would South Carolina ever beat Alabama? The answer again was yes. On September 29, 2001, the 15th-ranked Gamecocks rallied from 12 points down in the final nine minutes to beat the Crimson Tide 37-36.

Petty completed 19 of 33 passes for 291 yards, including touchdown passes of 43 yards to Brian Scott, 9 yards to Ryan Brewer, and 7 yards to tight end Rod Trafford for the game winner with just 2:18 left to play. It was the only reception of the year for Trafford.

THE GAME OF MY LIFE
BY PHIL PETTY

I remember it was a day game. We got up pretty early, but didn't spend a lot of time with meetings or talking. We went to the stadium—just a beautiful day. Then the game began; Alabama came out and went down early and scored. I think Tyler Watts ran for a career high that day (162 yards). They had a little option package they had put in that was pretty good against our defense with that three-man front. Tyler was a heck of a player, tough. He was executing the offense to a 'T' there.

I remember sitting on the bench in the second quarter and getting the guys together, saying, "We knew this was going to be tough. This is Alabama, boys. This ain't somebody that's going to roll out and get intimidated by us being 4-0. They came here to win this game."

For most of the game, we trailed. We were kind of back and forth there; it was just a game of frustration. We were close on some things but didn't convert. Then they were hitting on all points. The biggest part of the game was the fourth quarter. They had gone up 36-24. I think there were nine minutes left. We were getting the ball back—we had to score. We had to go answer, and it had to happen right then.

I told the guys on the sideline to focus on their jobs. Don't worry about what the left tackle is doing if you're the right tackle. Don't worry about what the front's doing if you're the split end. Don't worry about what the fullback's doing if you're the tailback. Just do your job. I said if we could go out there and execute our jobs, we'd do well enough to win the game. They wouldn't stop us. We'd stopped ourselves a few times—we just needed to focus on what we were doing.

So we went out and I remember we were in an empty package. We were spreading the field. They were mixing up zone and blitz on me. I just took what they gave me. If they blitzed, boom; I got rid of it. If they dropped out, I was going to find a hole, go down, and score. We held them. Defense did a good job, got the ball back.

We went down again and ran a little play-action pass. All week the guy in the flat had been open in practice. But they actually double-teamed him, and Rodney Trafford was one on one on a little stick round and did a good job of sticking his guy coming out, and we converted it. It was just a little 6-yard route. He's got an option where he can turn in or out. The guy had inside leverage on him. So he did the old basketball fake inside and came outside, and when he did, I threw it on time and converted the touchdown.

After that, the defense came back out and held them. Then came the best feeling: coming back on the field, right in front of our student section, knowing there were only about 20 seconds left and that we were going to take a knee. That's probably one of the highlights of our time in that stadium: knowing it was the first time in school history that we'd beaten a traditional powerhouse like Alabama and, more importantly, that we were now 5-0.

It was an emotional game. We were hugging afterward. But the guy I went to find was Tyler Watts. We hugged each other. I said to him—I'll never forget—"Man, you played a hell of a game."

He said, "No, bullshit, you did."

THE AFTERMATH

After beating Kentucky 42-6 the next week, the ninth-ranked Gamecocks fell to Arkansas 10-7 on October 13 in Little Rock, which Petty called a "hornet's nest." South Carolina rebounded to beat Vanderbilt to become bowl eligible and then, after a seven-point loss at Tennessee, downed Wofford before being annihilated 54-17 by Florida in Columbia.

But the Gamecocks would win their final two games, beating Clemson 20-15 in Columbia and then edging Ohio State 31-28 for the second straight year in the Outback Bowl.

All week, Petty said, the Buckeyes either said or implied the previous year's loss was a fluke and that their team was ready for redemption.

"So it turned into a pretty nasty pregame talk," he said. "I think the year before they felt like they got pushed around by an inferior team. I think they felt like they were the better team and that they were going to beat us. But obviously they were not successful."

But Petty was, ending his career with a victory over Clemson and following that with a second straight bowl victory.

"That's something any quarterback will tell you: if you can do that, you've done something important, because they don't give those things out. Bowl games, they're not free. If they were, shoot, everybody would have a bunch of them," Petty said.

"First of all, it's hard to win enough games to get there, and then once you're there, you're playing a team that has won national championships. To beat them twice, that's about as rewarding as you can get.

"And coming from where we were, I don't think I realized it until a couple years later what we had actually done. For that university and for the coaches and players that were involved, there's a lot to be proud of and a lot to be said for it."

Chapter 22

ERIK KIMREY

THE YOUNG LIFE OF ERIK KIMREY

Erik Kimrey, a onetime walk-on and seventh-string quarterback, is probably one of the most improbable heroes in more than a century of South Carolina football. The son of a coach, Kimrey decided to turn down an appointment at the Naval Academy to try the arduous (and thankless) route of walking on at South Carolina.

At Dutch Fork High School, Kimrey's father, Bill, ran the spread offense and threw the ball nearly every down. Along the way, the younger Kimrey eclipsed a few records but drew little attention from major schools.

"I didn't have the strongest arm," Kimrey said. "My only Division I offer was the Naval Academy. They ran the flex-bone option, which was not suited for my style of quarterback. I was more of a pocket passer."

But he decided to go to Annapolis anyway. He was planning to major in engineering and "make a lot of money." Then he changed his mind—after a nudge from his girlfriend, now wife, Erica Russell.

"She said, 'When have you ever been about financial things? You've been about doing what your heart tells you to do,'" Kimrey said. "I knew that one day I wanted to coach. So I thought going to a school like South Carolina would be a better spring board for that."

So Kimrey contacted coach Brad Scott, who politely told Kimrey to come in. Scott told Kimrey the coaches would treat him as a scholarship player, adding, "If you basically don't fall on your face, we'll put you on scholarship after a year."

Scott never lived up to that promise for the simple reason he wasn't around in 1999. After the Gamecocks finished 1-10, the lone win a season-opening 38-20 victory over Ball State, Scott was fired.

Enter the legendary Lou Holtz.

THE SETTING

With Holtz's arrival, Kimrey was shoved to the back of the quarterback line. He was the seventh-string quarterback in an injury-plagued 0-11 year in which Holtz played six quarterbacks in his run-oriented attack. Kimrey was not one of them.

"I knew I had a mountain to climb if I was ever going to play," he said.

But Kimrey insisted he never second-guessed his decision. What he lacked in talent, he made up for in brains and maturity and perspective.

"I think God graced me with a bit of ability to see the big picture. Today it's rare that kids know their limitations. I think I understood mine," he said.

"I saw some of these guys and said, these guys are a lot stronger and faster than I am; this is going to take me some time. So I think I was patient. It was frustrating at times. But at I kept a pretty level head about it."

For his first two years, Kimrey bided his time running the scout team offense, mimicking the next opponent's offense to help the defense prepare, a necessary if not glamorous part of college football. Kimrey used it as a learning experience.

"That was the best thing in the world for me," he said. "I really had some success over there and was able to throw the ball decently against some really good cornerbacks, a lot of guys playing in the

Erik Kimrey. *Photo provided by Collegiate Images/South Carolina*

pros right now—Sheldon Brown, Andre Goodman, Arturo Freeman, Willie Offord, Kalimba Edwards.

"And in the scout team setting it was more relaxed, because if you mess up, good job defense. And so I was able to kind of relax and just have fun and try to be somewhat of a leader over there."

The elder Holtz noticed. In a presage of Kimrey's future, Holtz called Kimrey aside one day at practice.

"I was the seventh-string guy and he said, 'Do you want to coach one day?' I said, 'Yes sir.' He asked, 'What level do you want to coach, high school or college?' I said I wasn't sure," Kimrey recalled. "He told me, 'If you want to be a college football coach, you come see me.'"

But that was the future; Kimrey was focused on the present and liked what he saw when, in 2000, the elder Holtz allowed his son, Skip, the offensive coordinator, to run more of a spread attack on offense. In Kimrey's words, he "loosened the reins."

"I was able to flourish a little bit more in a system like that, that I was more comfortable with, something I had run in high school, where I could distribute the ball. I was able to earn the backup quarterback job," Kimrey said.

While quarterback Phil Petty was a perfect fit for the spread, the other quarterbacks—Kimrey not included—struggled to grasp the system. They all knew the battle wasn't for the starting job but for No. 2.

"I was able to maybe make some decent decisions and get the ball in the guys' hands, and coming out of spring, I was No. 2. I think that they were hoping they could bring someone [else] in to be the No. 2 guy in the fall, but that didn't work out," Kimrey said. "So I was kind of two by default."

South Carolina had signed Dondrial Pinkins, a 6-foot-2, 240-pounder whom Kimrey said he once saw throw the ball 75 yards—over the upright.

"The strongest arm I've ever seen, and a good athlete," Kimrey said. "It was a no-brainer if he could do it mentally because he was just a freshman. He was a smart guy but had to learn it all."

Pinkins actually won the backup job before injuring his knee in two-a-days. So Kimrey was back at Petty's backup.

"I was in the right place at the right time," Kimrey said. "When you look back at it, it's just amazing, all the things that had to happen for that one situation to occur. It's just funny."

In what was an amazing turn of events, South Carolina had not only snapped its 21-game losing streak but was 3-0—including a 21-10 win over No. 9 Georgia—and on the cusp of the national rankings when No. 25 Mississippi State came to Columbia.

The Bulldogs were led by a defense that included future NFL player Fred Smoot and defensive coordinator Joe Lee Dunn, an ex-defensive coordinator at South Carolina under Joe Morrison known for his aggressive blitzing schemes.

When the day was done, however, the Gamecocks had prevailed 23-19, thanks in part to Kimrey, who went into the game battling for the backup role with converted wide receiver Carlos Spikes.

THE GAME OF MY LIFE
BY ERIK KIMREY

That week, we weren't sure who was going to come in if Petty got hurt. It was kind of based on the situation. But they did have a little package for Carlos to do some athletic things. But I had gotten some work, too.

I prepared as if I had to play. In the back of my mind, I didn't think I would play. So I was just going about what I normally would do in a game, signaling a lot of plays in and trying to stay in tune with what they were doing, and trying to help Phil as much as I could.

Phil was probably having the game of his career. What people don't realize is Phil threw for 305 yards against a very good defense, which was the most he ever threw for. But we were down 19-10 with eight minutes to go. We went down and kicked a field goal and stopped them and got the ball back.

I was sitting on the sideline watching. I was into the game but really not expecting I was going to go in. We were going down the field; it was third-and-10, and Phil scrambled and laid one up to James Adkisson, who jumped up over Fred Smoot, getting it down at the 25-yard line.

We were first-and-10 and they decided they're going to bring the house down. They were playing zero man. They were locked up, bringing more guys than we could block. So it was "catch it and get rid of it" for Phil.

It was third-and-10 again, and there were about four minutes left. A guy came off the edge untouched. Phil broke his initial tackle, rolled to the right, and laid one up out of bounds. As he was throwing the ball, somebody clipped him underneath and he landed on his ankle wrong.

I was looking at the ball, then I looked back and I saw Phil trying to get up and falling down. I was like, Uh-oh. Then he tried again and he fell down, and that's when it hit me that I better get my helmet on. So I grabbed my helmet. They called an official timeout and our trainers went out there. Phil couldn't get up.

I grabbed a ball. I was probably five yards away from Kevin Sides, who was a walk-on quarterback at the time. I threw about two or three passes about five yards. I hadn't thrown the ball since halftime.

Todd Fitch, who was our receiver coach, comes up to me—Skip was up in the box—and he said, "What do you like, what do you feel comfortable with?" I said to throw 18; 18 was the number where our outside guys ran a fade. I said, "They've been pressing. Let me just lay one up and see what happens." He said okay.

I could see him talking to Skip over the headphones. Then coach Lou Holtz came up to me and said, "Erik, what do you like?"

I said, "Coach, let's just throw the fade."

"You like it?" he said, and I said, "Yeah, let's do it."

So we got a little huddle together; there was no timeout. So it happened quickly and Coach Fitch said he wanted everybody to run vertical: "We're running 18." Normally on 18, the two inside receivers run a little quick out. But he told everyone to go vertical because there was no safety. He said, "Erik, pick the best matchup and let it go."

Honestly, I didn't have time to think. It was fourth-and-10. I didn't have time to think about the gravity of the situation: that there were 85,000 people in the stands, that we were 3-0 playing the 25th-ranked team in the country, that we were down by six points with three minutes to go into the game. None of that stuff entered my mind.

What entered my mind was, "Let's find the best matchup and lay it up and give somebody a chance." And so I trotted onto the field and I really wasn't that nervous. I got in the shotgun. I just called the cadence. Before the play started, I looked to see what kind of matchups I had. I saw James Adkisson against Fred Smoot. Then I saw Jermale Kelly on their other DB, who was a good player but not Fred Smoot, and Jermale was probably our best fundamental receiver. So it was a no-brainer.

The problem was Jermale was all the way to the field so it would be a longer throw. But I thought, I'm just going to lay it up and give him a shot. And so I raised my foot. I called the cadence. The ball was snapped.

I didn't even get the laces. I just caught it. We were taught to just catch it in the shotgun and let it go—it's called quick game. If you have the laces, you had them. If you don't, you don't. At that moment, there was no time to get the laces.

As I caught it, I was looking at Jermale. I saw that he was getting jammed a little bit. I needed to put more air on that ball to give him a chance to come out of the jam. When I initially let it go I thought it might have been a bit too far, because I wasn't sure how clean he was going to come out of that jam.

Well, he came out of there pretty clean, and he made an unbelievable catch. I'd put it in a pretty decent spot right on the goal line, right by the pylon. It hit his arm or shoulder and it bounced into his other arm and the DB never saw it. He was right there but he never saw it come down. Jermale made an unbelievable play.

When I saw that he caught it and that the official had thrown up the touchdown sign, my first thought was that it was way too good to be true. I looked around to make sure there were no flags. Actually, on the replay—I've seen the replay before—I jump up in the air and do the touchdown sign and then I look to my left and to my right and behind me to make sure there's no flag. As soon as I realized there were no flags, I sprinted toward the end zone.

I wasn't able to process the crowd. I was just thinking how what had happened was unbelievable. I ran down to the end zone to hug somebody. By the time I got there, there was nobody there. They were all hugging each other and moving away. So I think I high-fived a fan and went to the sideline.

One of the cool things was Phil Petty was the first one there waiting for me. He was limping, could barely walk. But he was that kind of guy. As soon as I got to the sideline he gave me a big hug. That's when I got nervous.

We made the extra point and it was 20-19. Then the reality of the situation set in on me. I realized that if we won that game, it was going to be something special, something people would talk about all year. So then I got nervous. I was like, "Come on guys, let's hang on."

And we were able to hang on.

THE AFTERMATH

As he sat on the sideline drinking some water, assistant coach Buddy Pough came over to Kimrey and kissed him on the cheek and his headset got caught in Kimrey's facemask.

"That was kind of funny," Kimrey said.

When the gun sounded, the first person to reach Kimrey was his brother, Kyle.

"It was just an unbelievable day," Kimrey said. Kimrey would do a blizzard of interviews, with dozens of reporters and cameras taking in his every word. He later ate dinner with his family and signed autographs at a local restaurant as ESPN broadcasted his game-winning throw.

"It was just kind of a surreal moment for my entire family," he said. "Really, when I graduated and was done playing, it was a memory that I knew I would always cherish. So it was a great day, a lot of fun for my entire family."

Kimrey had two years left, but that touchdown was his moment. He would play sparingly, but along the way he would help tutor Pinkins as well as another talented quarterback, Corey Jenkins, who wound up playing linebacker in the NFL.

"I felt my senior year I would have another shot. So I worked hard and trained for that," Kimrey said. "But I didn't get to play as much as I would have liked, but I have no regrets. It was nothing but a positive experience."

Chapter 23

DOMINIC FUSCI

THE YOUNG LIFE OF DOMINIC FUSCI

Dominic Fusci grew up in Greenwich Village in the 1930s and early 1940s, a memorable time in New York City to be sure.

"I was fortunate to be in New York," Fusci said. "I was the oldest of three in an Irish-Italian family. We were the only family in New York on St. Paddy's day that had corn beef and cabbage and spaghetti and meatballs."

Fusci remembers being involved in athletics from a young age.

"Playing fields were so few in New York that all my high school football games were played at Ebbets Field," Fusci remembers. "They'd start games at noon on Saturday and there would be four games played.

"I played for Manuel Training [High School], which sounds like a penitentiary, and maybe it should have been. In the summer, we'd go across to Prospect Park and get to Flatbush Avenue, where Ebbets Field was. There was this big metal door. We'd bang on the door and say 'Gus, Gus let us in. It's Fusci, Manuel Training.' He'd let us in and we'd be in the locker room with the Dodgers. They'd say, 'Hey kids, how you guys doing?'"

Fusci was a standout at Manuel Training High and was selected All-New York and All-Metro. College scouts began calling.

Fusci had an appointment with a coach at the Naval Academy during a coaching convention at the Hotel New Yorker when a chance encounter with South Carolina coach Rex Enright changed his future forever.

"I walked into the hotel and the newspaper reporters were talking to Coach Enright and they said, 'Here comes the kid now,'" Fusci remembers. "He stops me and says, 'I've heard a lot of good reports about you. I'd like to talk to you about the University of South Carolina.' I said, 'I'd love to, but I've got an appointment with the Naval Academy coach right now. If you don't mind, I'll see him right now and I'll see you later.'

"Being a kid from New York, I didn't want to go to the Naval Academy and deal with regulations and people telling me what to do. So I decided to go down to South Carolina. I took the bus and stopped off at North Carolina State first. Back then, they would try you out for two or three days. N.C. State offered a scholarship, but I went on down to South Carolina and that's where I decided to sign. I'm glad it turned out the way it did. It was the best move I could have made."

THE SETTING

Football came easily to Fusci at South Carolina, but what didn't come easily was adjusting to Southern accents.

"I'd never been any farther south than New Jersey," Fusci said. "I get down there and have these two roommates from South Carolina. I would ask them, 'What timezit?' They'd look at each other and say, 'What did he say?' I felt like I was in a foreign country, or maybe even another planet."

Like all incoming players in those days, Fusci had to play on the freshman team for a year before he could be eligible for the varsity.

"The first game I played in freshman college football was against Georgia and Charley Trippi," Fusci said. "We beat them 14-7. The last game I played, I was with the Philadelphia Eagles against the

Chicago Cardinals with Charley Trippi and beat them something like 64-14. So I started with Charley and I ended with Charley."

When Fusci moved up to the varsity in 1942, he settled right in as a starter on the line on both offense and defense. His first game on the varsity came against defending national champion Tennessee, and would generate one of many stories that characterized Fusci's career as one of South Carolina's most colorful athletes.

"My first game, we're playing Tennessee and I'm a sophomore and just about everybody else was a senior," Fusci said. "I had never chewed tobacco in my life. All the southern guys are chewing. So I took a bite out of it. I was going around acting tough and spitting. I came down on the kickoff and some guy hit me and the tobacco went down my throat. I got in the huddle and I'm groaning. They said, 'Get out of the huddle. We can't hear the plays.' So we had the lonesome tackle a long time before [Army coach] Red Blaik had the lonesome end.

"I line up across from the Tennessee guys, and they're like, 'Hey, this guy is having a heart attack.' My teammate Lou Sossamon says, 'Nah, he ain't having no heart attack. He's been acting like that ever since that dog bit him on Monday.'

"They were looking out for me. They didn't want to mess with me. Finally, after about three or four plays, I stuck my hand down my throat and threw it up into a towel. That's the last time I chewed tobacco."

From that inauspicious beginning, Fusci developed into a star for the Gamecocks. In 1943, he would anchor one of the best defensive football teams in the country, and it was a game during that season that stands out to Fusci as the most memorable of his career.

THE GAME OF MY LIFE
BY DOMINIC FUSCI

We had lost to North Carolina right before we played Wake Forest. That North Carolina game was the only one I missed. I was being transferred from Naval ROTC to the Naval Air Corps and had to miss it.

Anyway, I missed that game and North Carolina beat us. Here we were getting ready to play Wake Forest, and they were a better team than North Carolina. Back then, we played Wake Forest in Charlotte, North Carolina, on Thanksgiving Day. I was still mad as heck about the North Carolina game, and I really wanted to play well because this was the last game of the year and maybe my last game ever, since I was about to go into the Navy and off to war.

But let me tell you about how good we were on defense that year. Before that North Carolina game, we were allowing 22 yards in total offense and two first downs a game. Wake Forest had a good team and they looked like they were on their way to the Orange Bowl. All they had to do was beat us, and they were in.

We went out there and played them and just dominated the whole game. I blocked a couple punts that day and recovered a fumble and we beat them 13-2. The only way they scored was our guy was kicking from his end zone and he kicked the ball over his head and it went out of bounds for a safety. I could have killed him.

But they couldn't do anything, and we scored a couple touchdowns and took control of the game. They made some first downs, but that was about it. We were just a really good defensive team and we proved it that day against Wake Forest.

THE AFTERMATH

With the world at war, 1943 was an interesting year in college football.

Some schools didn't have enough available players to field teams. Many schools, South Carolina and Wake Forest included, had to fill out their schedule against military teams, which featured older, tougher players—men who were about to go, or had been, to war.

Other than a 21-6 loss to North Carolina, the Gamecocks' only loss that season was a 13-7 setback at the hands of a team representing the 175th Infantry.

Wake Forest, which would enter the South Carolina game with a 4-4 record, got roughed up by teams from Camp Davis and Greensboro Air Force Base.

By all accounts, South Carolina's 13-2 Thanksgiving Day victory over Wake Forest was a defensive struggle. The Gamecocks shut down Wake Forest's running game, holding the Deacons to 24 yards rushing. Wake managed 164 yards passing, but South Carolina's defense forced six turnovers on four fumble recoveries and two interceptions.

It was the last game of the season for both teams. Wake Forest finished 4-5, while South Carolina finished 5-3.

Just like any number of other athletes at other schools, Dominic Fusci's career at South Carolina was interrupted by World War II.

After the 1943 season, he went off to war, serving on PT boats and PT tenders in the Pacific Theatre. And even though he was at war, Fusci remained a character of the first order.

"During the war I received a letter from the Washington Redskins informing me that I was their third-round draft choice," Fusci said.

"I went to my commanding officer and told him I needed the next plane or boat out of there because they wanted to speak to me in Washington. He said, 'How come I didn't get the letter?' I said, 'Well, it wasn't addressed to you.' He said, 'Let me see that letter, Fusci.' He looked at it and saw Washington Redskins and said, 'Get your butt out of here, Fusci, and get back on that damn boat.' As I was walking out the door, he said, 'Congratulations.'"

However, Fusci never played for the Redskins. After the war, he returned to South Carolina in 1946 to finish his college career.

"It was an easy decision," Fusci said. "The Redskins wanted to pay me $175 a game. With what I was getting from South Carolina, I couldn't afford to take the pay cut."

After finishing at South Carolina and a brief career in the fledging days of pro football, Fusci returned to Columbia, South Carolina, where he worked as a sales rep for Southern Radio, a division of RCA.

Over the years, he kept his hand in with sports, officiating football and basketball games, boxing matches, and umpiring baseball.

To this day, he's proud of his Gamecock roots.

"USC is not only part of my life, it's part of my name," Fusci is fond of saying. "Just take USC and add an F on the front and an I on the back."

Chapter 24

GORDON BECKHAM

THE YOUNG LIFE OF GORDON BECKHAM

Gordon Beckham grew up in Atlanta in the shadows—literally as well as figuratively—of Georgia Tech and Georgia. Beckham was a Bulldog fan, and more than two decades later his son would go on to play baseball for Georgia in the 2006 College World Series.

If the elder Beckham had ever been a fan of South Carolina, he decided on September 30, 1978, that he would never play for the Gamecocks after his official visit to Columbia. While on that trip, he watched his future alma mater defeat Georgia 27-10 at Williams-Brice Stadium.

"The one thing I knew when I left that weekend was that I would not go to the University of South Carolina," Beckham said. "I just left with the feeling that that was one place I wouldn't go to. I could mark it off my list."

Beckham soon erased that mark, however, when South Carolina assistant—and future Georgia head coach—Ray Goff started recruiting him.

"If it had not been for him," Beckham said, "I think it'd be safe to say I would not have gone to South Carolina."

Beckham might have wound up at Georgia, North Carolina, Auburn or Tennessee, who were all pursing the Westminster High School star. But Beckham couldn't say no to Goff.

"He's just the best salesman in the world. I grew up being a University of Georgia fan. Of course, he was a very successful quarterback at the University of Georgia," Beckham said.

"I had heard about him and followed him during my high school years. He was just someone I looked up to and he made a really strong impression on me and became a very close friend during that recruiting process. He closed the sale."

To this day, Beckham can't put his finger on what exactly he disliked while on his official visit to Columbia, South Carolina. His best speculation is that perhaps there was no "personal connection" with the Gamecocks until Goff started recruiting him.

"He just was very conscientious and very disciplined in staying in touch with me. We related as quarterbacks, and I guess the Georgia connection had something to do with it," Beckham said. "I think if he had been at Georgia and done the same thing I'd have gone to Georgia."

THE SETTING

Beckham didn't play much as a freshman in 1979 as the Gamecocks recovered from a season-opening 28-0 loss at North Carolina to win five straight games en route to an 8-4 record and a trip to the Hall of Fame Bowl.

Beckham's chances of playing certainly weren't enhanced after he ruptured two discs in his back while lifting weights in preparation for his first college season.

"I think that had an impact on my ability to compete the way I was used to competing. I didn't throw the ball well with this back issue," he said. "It continued to get worse and worse."

Back problems continued to plague him throughout his sophomore season, and after South Carolina lost to Pittsburgh 37-9

Gordon Beckham. *Photo provided by Collegiate Images/South Carolina*

in the Gator Bowl, Beckham decided it was time to have his back surgically repaired.

"I probably should have red-shirted that year or taken more time to recover," Beckham said. "But I really felt it was time to play. I was tired of sitting on the bench and not playing. So I really rushed the rehab. I came back and didn't miss any time my junior year."

As Beckham looked back, he said one of the highlights of his career was playing with top-flight players, including Heisman Trophy winner George Rogers and tight end Willie Scott, both of whom went on to be first-round NFL draft picks.

After missing spring practice because of his back, Beckham came into the fall of 1981 believing the quarterback job was up in the air, although he felt he was "behind the eight ball" because he missed spring ball.

Beckham and Terry Bishop shared the job early on during the season before Beckham took over the starting role exclusively. South Carolina lost three of its first five, including a 42-28 loss at home to Pittsburgh and Dan Marino, who threw a school-record six touchdown passes.

But Beckham rallied South Carolina from a 28-0 deficit in the second half and then led the Gamecocks to wins at Kentucky and back home against Virginia before they took a ride to Tobacco Road to face third-ranked North Carolina.

The Tar Heels had won 10 straight games dating back to 1980, and 21 of their last 22, and were more than a two-touchdown favorite to handle the Gamecocks, who in their last two trips to Chapel Hill had had lost 17-0 and 28-0.

But September 24, 1981, was South Carolina's day—and Beckham's. He completed his first 14 passes—a school record—and was 16 of 17 for 195 yards and one touchdown in the 31-13 victory.

The only incompletion came on an offensive pass interference call, which then was statistically counted as an incompletion against Beckham, whose 94.1 completion percentage remains a school record.

GORDON BECKHAM

THE GAME OF MY LIFE
BY GORDON BECKHAM

I remember it was a cold, overcast day—great weather for a football player. But for fans, it wasn't a very pretty day. It's hard to describe because I do remember it well. It was a somewhat surreal feeling in that I just felt we were going to win that game. I just felt very confident about the game and our opportunities in the game.

I think one of North Carolina's key defensive guys was hurt. I didn't understand it but they played a lot of man coverage that day, and they were really pressing our wide receivers very close to the line of scrimmage.

We checked off a lot that day and threw the ball down the field. The guys were getting open and I guess a blind hog will find an acorn every now and again. I was throwing the ball well. It was just one of those days that you felt very confident, like we were going to win, and we did.

Without question, it was probably the best day for us that year. We just played very well in all areas of the game. It wasn't just the offense. The defense played well. I think we blocked a punt.

Other than just having a different feeling about our opportunities for success during warm-ups, I can't put my finger on anything tangible. And I think North Carolina helped us a lot, the way they played that day.

It was (personally) a spectacular day. It was hard to believe the way things fell into place for us. My teams had had a lot of success in high school, but up until that point, I had not experienced as much satisfaction with any level of play as I did that day.

There were just great performances all the way around. We had time to throw the ball. North Carolina was in man coverage quite a bit. They were blitzing quite a bit. Our guys were able to get open and it just went really well.

I remember one play. It was third-and-1 or third-and-2 and their cornerback was about two yards off the line of scrimmage with

Horace Smith. He was on the wide side of the field. We checked off and we went deep. Horace got open for a 40- or 50-yard completion.

It was a very unorthodox check. You typically wouldn't make that check in that situation. You'd run a more conservative play. But we went down the field. He got open and made the catch. The throw was there. It was that kind of day. If things could go right for us, they went right. We were executing almost flawlessly.

I remember walking off the field with my stepfather after the game. It was very quiet. It was just the two of us. There had been a lot of media attention and interviews in the locker room, so I guess I'd been one of the last to leave. I just remember him saying, "You're probably not going to have a game like this next week, but it does not impact who you are as a person. You're the same person today as you're going to be next week." I'll just never forget that.

THE AFTERMATH

The next week, South Carolina returned home to beat North Carolina State 20-12, running its record to 6-3 with games against Pacific and Clemson, which would go on to win the national championship, and then end the regular season with a trip to Honolulu to face Hawaii.

The Gamecocks looked like a sure bet to wind up in the Peach Bowl, but Pacific, which had lost to South Carolina 37-0 a year earlier, stunned the Gamecocks 23-21—the first of three straight losses to end the season.

"I don't know what happened in that Pacific game," Beckham said. "It was just a debacle."

After Clemson beat South Carolina 29-13, Beckham broke his thumb in practice when he hit a teammate's helmet. Hawaii beat the Gamecocks 33-10 amid not only the distractions of Beckham's injury and being in Hawaii, but also the questions about the future of coach Jim Carlen.

"At that time, I think there was beginning to be some controversy with Coach Carlen and whether or not he was going to be back," Beckham said.

One week later, on December 12, 1981, Carlen was fired. He was later replaced by Richard Bell, who lasted one year—the Gamecocks were 4-7, losing five of their last six games, including a stunning 28-23 loss to Furman in 1982.

"I don't really have any fond memories at all of my senior year," Beckham said.

His career over, Beckham was ready to move on, graduating from the University of South Carolina's highly regarded International Business Studies program. He returned home to Atlanta and went into business and never looked back.

"I knew football was over at that point," he said. "I had had enough of football. I had just had enough."

Chapter 25

WARREN MUIR

THE YOUNG LIFE OF WARREN MUIR

Warren Holmes Muir grew up in a large family—he was the youngest of five children until his brother, Peter, was born when he was 15—in a typical industrial city in the northeast. Fitchburg, Massachusetts, which is just 10 miles from the New Hampshire state line and 50 miles northwest of Boston, was a blue-collar town on the Nashua River. The river provided power for the paper and textile mills, as well as for the machine and tool companies, that were the community's chief employers. It was a town of immigrants, including those of Irish, Italian, Finnish, and Welsh descent. Muir's father, Allen, worked for a local paper company.

"We lived in a blue-collar neighborhood in West Fitchburg where most neighbors knew each other and watched out for one another," Muir said. "Young kids played outside year round and enjoyed unorganized pickup sports games—baseball and football in local fields and pastures, and basketball at outdoor school playgrounds."

Muir's flag football team won three city championships. Growing up with three older brothers and an older sister, young Warren would tag along with his siblings when they went to play whatever sport was in season.

"Playing with the older kids," he said, "taught me to tough things out versus quitting and being a spectator."

Muir's parents supported their children's interest in sports, taking them to games and practices as well as taking the time to play catch or hit fly balls or grounders to them. Both, Muir recalled, also "preached good sportsmanship, hard play, honesty, and team play, lessons that I've never forgotten and for which I will always be thankful."

But education was equally important in the Muir household. At Fitchburg High School, Muir said the guidance counselors emphasized the importance of good grades and extracurricular activities—beyond sports—for students hoping to land a scholarship. Muir took the message to heart, knowing his parents couldn't afford to send him to college.

"So it was up to me to either get a job when I finished high school or get a scholarship if I wished to continue my education," he said.

Muir caught the eye of one college recruiter as a high school freshman. Before a track meet in the winter of 1962, Muir said he was told George Terry, a defensive assistant on coach Paul Dietzel's staff at Army, was in the school office and wanted to talk with him.

"I was ecstatic," Muir recalled. "I had played varsity football as a freshman and had some press coverage. The West Point staff would clip out the write ups, highlight my name and stats, stamp 'the Black Knights of the Hudson have their eyes on you' on the clippings and mail them to 80 Appleton Circle, my address.

"Now a coach was in the school asking for a visit. I was 14 at the time and was overwhelmed."

Muir played halfback on offense, and defensive back and linebacker on defense, earning all-state honors and being named to several all-star teams. He also ran track, setting a school and state class B record in the shot put as a senior.

Off the field, Muir worked odd jobs to make money, cutting grass or picking blueberries in the summer and shoveling snow in the winter. For two summers he worked at a pool at a local golf course.

Warren Muir. *Photo provided by Collegiate Images/South Carolina*

Along the way, he also graduated with honors while serving as class president his final two years.

Many schools were interested in Muir as graduation neared, although mostly from the northeast. But Muir said he was "pretty well hooked on West Point" after his visits with Terry and Dietzel, who had coached LSU to the 1958 national title.

Muir also got to see two Army-Navy games, where he saw, among others, quarterback Roger Staubach, who would go on to win the Heisman Trophy. So it was off to West Point for Muir, where he played football and ran track.

But the next spring Dietzel was gone, having accepted a job at the University of South Carolina. Muir followed the coach after his freshman year at West Point, enrolling in the engineering school at South Carolina. He was red shirted in 1966. Before transferring, Muir had never been farther south than Philadelphia.

THE SETTING

His first year in Columbia required a few adjustments. First, he was newly married, having walked down the aisle a few months earlier. Then he dislocated his shoulder during preseason practice. After that, it would frequently pop out not only while practicing, but also while doing pushups or playing handball.

"It was so loose I could reset it myself," he said. "So I spent my first full year as a red shirt transfer briefly on the light duty 'red-cross' team—not too prestigious."

Among the assistants on Dietzel's staff were two coaches who would go on to bigger things: Lou Holtz and Sam Wyche.

"Little did I know then how they'd eventually succeed," Muir said.

Muir's father died in October at the age of 52. The loss was devastating for Muir.

"My grades suffered," Muir said, adding that he was put on academic probation. Terry asked Muir if he'd consider an easier major than engineering. But Muir said he was not ready to quit.

Eventually, Muir righted himself academically and would go on to graduate with a degree in civil engineering.

Muir also became a father his first year in Columbia with the birth of his son, Jeffrey, the first of four children. Amid all this, Muir also underwent surgery on his shoulder to keep it from repeatedly popping out. Spring practice passed without any problems for Muir and his shoulder.

The Gamecocks opened the 1967 season with a 34-3 win over Iowa State, with Muir coming on in the second half and rushing for 89 yards and two touchdowns. South Carolina followed that with wins over North Carolina and Duke but lost its last three games, finishing 5-5 and 4-2 in the ACC.

Muir finished with 805 yards rushing, including a career-best 164 yards against UNC. For his efforts Muir was named to the All-ACC team, which was honored in Greenville. So Muir and teammates Tim Bice and Don Somma made the drive, which took about twice as long as it should have because of ice and snow.

"Don and I did a lot of pushing during the three-hour ride while Tim managed to keep the car on the slippery road," Muir said. "The first person I saw and met when we walked into the ballroom of the Jack Tar Hotel was Clemson's legendary coach, Frank Howard.

"He was standing around the cocktail bar with the six Clemson players who had been selected after winning the conference title... He was a cordial, friendly showman and offered to buy us Gamecocks a drink at the open, free bar! Wanting to show our graciousness, we all obliged him and proceeded to have a very enjoyable evening listening to his yarns and sports stories."

On paper, 1968 was a forgettable year for the Gamecocks, who finished 4-6 (4-3 in the ACC). But Muir said the record wasn't indicative of the team's talent. But close losses—four of which were by seven points or less—proved to be the team's undoing.

As his senior year rolled around, Muir remembered the Gamecocks being pumped up, feeling the team had matured; it had a strong nucleus that included three solid recruiting classes. Also,

Muir said, South Carolina's freshman teams—freshmen were ineligible to play on the varsity at the time—went undefeated.

"Adding to the hype was that 1969 was the 'Year of the Rooster' according to the ancient Chinese lunar calendar," Muir said.

South Carolina opened the season with home wins over Duke and North Carolina but then stumbled at Georgia. The Gamecocks lost 41-19. Muir rushed for 136 yards but was not happy.

South Carolina rallied to beat N.C. State 21-16 the next week and edged Virginia Tech 17-16 in Blacksburg the following week on a 47-yard field goal in the final seconds by 5-foot-5 Billy Dupre, who had missed two earlier field goals.

Assistant coach Don "Scooter" Purvis got so excited in the coaches booth in the press box that he hyperventilated and was rushed to the hospital because observers thought he was having a heart attack. It turned out to be a false alarm.

After beating Maryland 17-0 to run their record to 5-1 and 4-0 in the ACC, the Gamecocks lost on the road to Florida State 34-9 and Tennessee 29-14. Muir rushed for 159 yards against the Volunteers.

But the Gamecocks rebounded the next week to beat Wake Forest 24-6, clinching the ACC title, which to this day remains the school's only conference title in football in more than 100 years.

The next week USC looked to clinch an undefeated ACC season against archrival Clemson in what would be the final game of coach Frank Howard's career.

THE GAME OF MY LIFE
BY WARREN MUIR

There was a lot of pregame hype. Clemson's record was 4-5 and they needed a 'W' to achieve a break-even season. They were determined to spoil our perfect ACC season despite that we had already earned the 1969 conference championship. After all, Clemson lost the ACC crown to N.C. State in 1968 by losing to USC. It was rumored that this was Frank Howard's last season as head coach. His 1969 squad was determined to send him out on a winning note.

For me it came down to having to live in South Carolina for the rest of my life, knowing I was involved with losing to Clemson three out of the four years I played—counting my red shirt year—versus winning the two most important ones, my junior and senior years.

Saturday, November 22, 1969 was the perfect day for a season-ending football game between South Carolina's two state teams with a rivalry dating back to the first game in 1896. The sky was blue and the weather cool. A gentle breeze brought movement to the national, state, and school flags flying throughout the "Cockpit." For the fifth time that season, an overflow crowd of fans filled the stadium, with the home crowd's garnet dominating the visitors' orange and purple.

In the first quarter, our defense shut down their offense. We scored on our first two possessions to lead 14-0 going into the second quarter. Our first drive went 74 yards in 14 plays, with Rudy Holloman dancing in for the 7-yard touchdown run. Our second drive covered 68 yards. I carried the ball the last three yards for the touchdown. In our previous nine games we had not scored a TD in the first quarter. We were excited.

On our third possession, early in the second quarter, we drove down and Billy DuPre kicked a 21-yard field goal. We were up 17-0 after our first three possessions. Was this going to be a runaway? Not yet. Clemson, led by running back Ray Yauger, mustered a nice drive to score. Then, after a blocked punt and a much shorter drive, Yauger scored again on a flare pass after faking into the line. What appeared to be a rout early was now a slim 17-13 lead. The Tigers had momentum as they went into the locker room to prep for the second half of play.

I can't tell you what was said in the Clemson locker room, but we got an earful about letting down, letting them block a punt, etc., and about playing the final 30 minutes as intensely as we had played the first 15. Would we?

They kicked off, and we chewed up about nine minutes driving to their 32. Tommy Suggs called a play that sent Rudy Holloman out of the backfield and down the right sideline. Tommy rolled right and found Holloman five yards behind Clemson's safety, hit him on the run, and Rudy high stepped the rest of the way into the end zone. Score: 24-13 following DuPre's extra point.

Both teams played solid defense after that, and we exchanged punts for the remainder of the third quarter and half of the fourth quarter. Recall that our punt protection had broken down earlier. We were faced with a fourth down after driving into Clemson territory midway through the final period. Could our punter, Billy Parker, pin them back deep? Would Clemson block another punt to give them a chance with good field position and enough time to score twice?

Parker caught the deep snap from center and started to run to his right: a fake punt! Then Parker, who'd played quarterback in high school, pulled up and threw a strike to Fred Zeigler for a vital first down. Not only did this successful trickery put us close enough for another field goal by DuPre, but also it allowed us to run down the clock, leaving Clemson little time to overcome our 14-point lead.

THE AFTERMATH

Muir rushed for 127 yards and one touchdown as part of a then-school record-setting 517-yard effort on offense. A week later Muir was named to the 1969 Kodak Football Coaches All-American team and later to the All-ACC squad, while Dietzel was named ACC coach of the year.

Muir would finish his career against West Virginia in the Peach Bowl. But South Carolina's performance was lackluster, losing 14-3 before 20,000-plus USC fans in a game Muir said is still called the "mud bowl" by the players because of the rain and cold.

"My performance was mediocre," he said. "I received a 'stinger' late in the second quarter and my neck stiffened up during the halftime break." As a result he played sparingly in the second half.

"That ended my football career at USC on a lower scale than I'd have preferred," he said, "but all in all, I consider the whole four-year experience quite satisfying."

Muir was picked by the New York Giants in the final round of the NFL draft but was cut during the preseason. Muir considered playing in the Canadian Football League but decided his football career had come to an end.

Muir worked as a construction manager for McCrory-Sumwalt after graduating and then with Michelin before joining Gillam & Associates, a general contractor in Aiken, where he has spent the last 20 years.

"Yogi Berra once said, 'When you come to the fork in the road, take it,'" Muir said. "It's impossible for me to remember all the many forks in my 'road' from West Fitchburg, Massachusetts, to Aiken. However, I can say with certainly that I have taken my fair share and won't look back."

Chapter 26

DICKIE HARRIS

THE YOUNG LIFE OF DICKIE HARRIS

Growing up in Point Pleasant Beach, New Jersey, Dickie Harris' first exposure to organized athletics came from baseball.

"Baseball is really where it all started for me," Harris said. "I was a big Yankees fan back when Mickey Mantle and Roger Maris were playing. Then I started with football in Pop Warner League when I was 12 or 13. The town probably only had about 5,000 people, but the sports programs in the area and all over the state were just excellent."

Harris showed great talent in every sport he tried, thanks in large part to his exceptional quickness.

"I think I was just gifted," he said. "I was always the fastest kid in the class and excelled right from the start. My mother and father were both athletic. My dad was a three-sport guy in high school."

By the time he got to high school, baseball went on the backburner for Harris and was replaced by football, basketball, and track and field.

"We had a great track team," he said. "We were state champs something like two years in a row. Nobody went out for baseball in high school. Everybody wanted to run track."

Dickie Harris. *Photo provided by Collegiate Images/South Carolina*

Harris' skills caught the eye of college scouts, and fortunately for South Carolina, the Gamecocks had an inside edge. Robert Harris, Dickie's older brother, had signed with the Gamecocks on a combination football-track scholarship four years earlier.

"My brother was actually faster than me as far as the 100-yard dash," Dickie said. "I think he ran a 9.8 100 in high school and a 20.9 220. And he was bigger than me. I was like 145 out of high school and he was like 6-1, 220. I'm 5-11. He scored the winning touchdown against Clemson his sophomore year. Then his junior year, in spring ball, he blew out his knee. That was it. But because of Robert, South Carolina knew about me and stayed in touch and recruited me. I just kind of followed him down there."

THE SETTING

Harris signed with the Gamecocks as a running back, but his lack of size led to a position switch after his freshman year.

"I was the starting running back, fastest guy on the team but really small," Harris said. "I weighed something like 152 pounds. I think I carried about 15 times in five games as a freshman.

"I always ended up blocking for the fullback, a 245-pound guy. It wasn't until I got to the spring that I got my break. They had me returning punts and kickoffs and I just had a phenomenal spring game and that started everything. I was still relatively small for a running back, but they needed defensive backs. So they put me over on defense at corner and my sophomore year, I won the corner spot. I still had the chance to return kicks and keep my hands on the ball."

Harris would prove to be a three-year starter at corner, and absolutely deadly in the return game. By his junior season, he was one of the Gamecocks' best players, and early in the year, he returned a punt for a touchdown against North Carolina.

When South Carolina went down to Georgia on October 31, 1970, he put his considerable skills on display.

THE GAME OF MY LIFE
BY DICKIE HARRIS

I think one of the reasons the Georgia game sticks out to me is that it was on TV and so many people saw it. It wasn't like today where nearly every game is televised. We were hardly ever on TV back then, so it was special, and it was a crazy game. I had a 96-yard kickoff returned for a touchdown and a 94-yard interception returned for a touchdown. Georgia was ranked and we were a big underdog, but we were beating them 21-3.

Mike Cavan was their starting quarterback and he got hurt. So all of a sudden, we've got this big lead and their quarterback is out of the game. I thought we had them. We all thought we had them. Then they brought in this guy by the name of Paul Gilbert, and he just had a phenomenal game. He was falling down as he threw passes and still completing them. All of a sudden, they came back, and the game tied. They went ahead, and then we regained the lead briefly in the fourth quarter, but in the end, they pulled away from us to win 52-34. The game was at Georgia, and they had a great crowd. Plus, it was really hot that day. I think maybe we just ran out of gas; I know I had after those two long runs.

We had a pretty good football team that year but we lost a lot of close games. We lost to Tennessee 20-18 on a field goal. We lost to Duke 42-38, and then to Georgia, 52-34, though we'd been beating them. All those games were winnable. It turned out to be a frustrating year. There were a lot of disappointments. Everybody would be so excited for a big part of the game, and then to lose it…I think maybe that was the start of the slide that year. You're in their back yard, you're beating them and all of a sudden you kind of end up giving it away.

THE AFTERMATH

South Carolina and Georgia did indeed put on a show for the Homecoming crowd of 57,391 at Sanford Stadium that day, as well as for a regional television audience.

Thanks to Harris' heroics, the Gamecocks raced out to a 21-3 lead. But when the Bulldogs turned to Gilbert at quarterback, they began to roll. Gilbert threw a 60-yard touchdown pass to tight end Billy Brice. Giving the Bulldogs their first lead of the game at 32-31 with 4:11 to play in the third quarter.

South Carolina came back to take a 34-32 lead early in the fourth quarter on a 36-yard field goal by Billy DuPre.

Georgia finally took the lead for good on a 10-yard touchdown run by Gilbert and a two-point conversion that put the Bulldogs ahead 40-34 with 8:41 to play in the game. The Bulldogs tacked on a couple of insurance scores, benefiting from Gamecock turnovers.

Still, what most people came away talking about were Harris' two dazzling, long-distance touchdowns.

After leaving South Carolina, Harris was faced with several professional football options.

The New York Jets drafted him in the fifth round, but he was also getting overtures from the Montreal Alouettes of the Canadian Football League.

"I went up to New York with all the draftees," Harris said. "I remember talking with [tight end] Rich Castor and some of the other Jets at the time. They were all pretty disgruntled with the pay structure. They were the lowest-paying franchise in the NFL. All the money was basically going to Joe Namath.

"Montreal flew me up twice, offered me more money, a bigger signing bonus. They were kissing my butt. They really wanted me. The Jets didn't seem to care whether I came or not. Back then, the money wasn't there, but the CFL had started making a push to sign Americans. They had signed [quarterback] Joe Theismann from Notre Dame the year before. The Jets offered me a $5,000 signing bonus and $15,000 a year. Montreal offered me a $15,000 signing bonus and $25,000 a year. And they wanted me. I flew into Montreal and it was like being in Europe. It was so beautiful, so gorgeous. It was like an international city. I said, 'This is such a cool place, I'm going to go.' I never looked back."

Harris had a Hall of Fame career in the CFL, playing on two Gray Cup Championship teams. He now works as an investment broker in British Columbia.

Harris still stays in touch with his Gamecock teammates, mostly by trading e-mails, and they keep him up to speed on the South Carolina program.

"I loved playing at South Carolina," Harris said. "That was a special time in my life that I'll always remember. I built a lot of friendships during my four years at South Carolina. My experience there was great and the fans were the best that I experienced anywhere, including professionally. I had a good career and really appreciated them being behind me, win or lose."

Chapter 27

ALSHON
JEFFERY

THE YOUNG LIFE OF
ALSHON JEFFERY

Alshon Jeffery's football career almost never got off the ground.

Growing up in an athletic family in St. Matthews, S.C., that included two sports-playing older brothers, Jeffery's first love was basketball.

While he dabbled with other sports, including football, basketball was his obsession.

"I used to play basketball every day," Jeffery said. "My older brothers [Ben and Darren] played football and basketball, so I wanted to do the same thing. But I always loved basketball. If it wasn't for basketball, there wouldn't have been football."

Jeffery dabbled with football in middle school, but didn't take it seriously. He was obsessed with basketball and was good enough to play on local AAU teams.

The 10th grade became a pivotal year in athletics for Jeffery.

"My 10th-grade year, the coach was on me all the time about football, kept nagging me," Jeffery said. "I was like, 'Ah, man I'm a basketball player,' but I went out there and gave it a shot. Next week, I quit and went back to basketball. Then I was back on the football field. I quit again."

Alshon Jeffery. *AP Images*

Jeffery may have irritated the football coaches by quitting twice, but they weren't foolish enough to give up on such a talent.

His freshman and sophomore years, Jeffery led Calhoun County High School to the first two of what would become four consecutive state championships in basketball.

The football team hoped he could perform similar magic for them.

"When I came back my junior year, I started making plays and we had a great season," Jeffery said. "We played Allendale-Fairfax in the first round of the playoffs and I had like four touchdowns and a bunch of unbelievable catches. That was what really made me change. I knew I could do it if I stuck to it and played hard. That summer, I quit playing basketball and stuck with football."

Jeffery started getting attention from college scouts, and he had his heart set on USC—the one in California, not the one in South Carolina.

"I was a big Reggie Bush fan," Jeffery said. "I really wanted to play for Southern Cal. They offered, and I committed to them without ever setting foot on campus."

Then Jeffery did a reality check.

"Me and my mom sat down and talked about financially how difficult it would be for her to come and visit me if I went to Southern Cal," he said. "So I made the best decision and decided on South Carolina."

Jeffery said another major factor in swaying his decision came when he talked to fellow South Carolina recruits DeVonte Holloman and Stephon Gilmore.

"We talked about it at the Under Armour -high school all-star] game and we sort of agreed that everybody else has already got their program set," Jeffery said. "We can come to South Carolina and change things and do things that have never been done before. I thought about that. Look at it, here we are today, and everybody's talking about South Carolina. I feel like we're a big part of the program being changed."

THE SETTING

Jeffery wasted no time making an impact at South Carolina.

His first season, he made several Freshman All-American teams after leading the Gamecocks in receptions with 46 catches for 763 yards and six touchdowns.

He remembers the Kentucky game, which was the seventh game of the 2009 season, as being pivotal.

"When I first got here, it was a change," Jeffery said. "I mean in high school, I didn't lift weights or anything. When I got to South Carolina, I just worked on getting stronger and learning the playbook. I knew I could make catches and make big plays. I just needed the opportunity. The opportunity came in the Kentucky game and the rest is history."

Jeffery caught seven passes for 138 yards and three touchdowns, including a highlight reel one-hander, in the Gamecocks' 28-26 over the Wildcats.

There would be no "sophomore slump" for Jeffery. On the contrary, he would stamp himself as one of the best wide receivers in the country.

The Gamecocks were on the improve as well, and after finishing 7-6 in 2009 South Carolina entered 2010 with high expectations.

The Gamecocks got off to a 3-1 start, with the only glitch coming in a 35-27 loss on the road to eventual national champion Auburn.

Next on the schedule was a game against undefeated defending national champion Alabama, which was riding a 19-game winning streak.

ESPN College GameDay was scheduled to be on hand. With the whole college football world watching, South Carolina had a chance to prove they belonged among the nation's best.

GAME OF MY LIFE

BY ALSHON JEFFERY

"There was just so much riding on it. I mean, everybody was thinking Alabama was unbeatable. I saw an interview with ESPN that week and I was just listening to all the talk of people saying they were cocky, they were going to make a repeat and nobody could beat them. They were unstoppable. Me and my teammates believed we could stop them. I don't even know if our coaches believed. But we believed. We had confidence we could beat them.

"Coming into the games, I'm always a little nervous, but I was more excited at that point, ready to get started. The first touchdown I had on [Alabama defensive back] Mark Barron, [Stephen] Garcia just made a great throw under pressure and I just made a great catch. As the game went along, we just got more and more comfortable making plays and our defense played huge for us. We combined to hold Trent Richardson and Mark Ingram to less than 100 yards rushing. That's what we needed.

"We made plays on crucial third downs. We just made the plays that we needed to make to win the game. When the game was going on, we were just concentrated on making plays, keeping drives alive. Whatever it takes to get it done, we need to get it done. We all came together to win the game.

"I made a lot of crucial catches on first down, second down, third down. I don't remember making any on fourth down, but I remember that last touchdown on a one-handed catch when the guy was all over me. That was probably the most crucial one.

"I wasn't nervous, but we just wanted to show the world what South Carolina football is about. That game probably let people know that our program was for real.

"In the locker room afterward, music was going, everybody was jumping around, coach [Steve] Spurrier was giving out game balls. It was just a locker room full of joy. I remember him telling us to go out and enjoy the next 24 hours and then we'll get back to it the next week.

"Any team can be beaten on any given day. On that given day, I think we were the No. 1 team in the nation. I think we would have beaten anybody on that day. We all played together as a team. We all had a great game. Coach Spurrier called all the right plays. Our defense played well. Coach [Ellis] Johnson and coach [Lorenzo] Ward did all the right things. I just think we were the best team in the country on that day."

THE AFTERMATH

South Carolina's 35-21 triumph over Alabama on Oct. 9, 2010 was a landmark victory in what would turn out to be a landmark season for the Gamecock program.

It was the Gamecocks' first victory over a team ranked No. 1 and propelled them to a nine-victory season and the school's first Southeastern Conference Eastern Division title.

Jeffery finished the game with seven receptions for 127 yards and two touchdowns.

For the season, he caught 88 passes for 1,517 yards and nine touchdowns while earning nearly consensus All-American honors. He was one of three finalists for the Biletnikoff Award, given annually to the nation's outstanding collegiate receiver.

He would play one more season for the Gamecocks and finished his career with 183 receptions for 3,042 yards and 23 touchdowns.

After making the decision to leave school a year early for the NFL, Jeffery was a first-round pick of the Chicago Bears.

"I have a lot of great memories from being a Gamecock," Jeffery said. "I remember me and [safety] D.J. Swearinger sitting in our living room watching our baseball team win the College World Series the first time. Then we sat in the same chairs and watched them do it again the next year. I will always be a diehard Gamecock for life. There are a lot of great memories."

At the top of the list is the victory over the Crimson Tide.

"I don't think it will probably hit us until we're in our 40s and we're done playing ball," Jeffery said. "We might talk about it after that. As of right now, it's pretty cool, but when we sit down with our kids and tell them what we did, that will be fun."

Chapter 28

MARCUS LATTIMORE

THE YOUNG LIFE OF MARCUS LATTIMORE

Like most gifted athletes, Marcus Lattimore played just a little bit of every sport growing up.

However, Lattimore recognized early on that sports like baseball and basketball were mere amusement for him. Football had his heart.

"I grew up in Duncan, S.C., and I started playing baseball, basketball and football when I was seven years old," Lattimore said. "I played everything up until seventh grade, and after seventh grade, I just stuck with football. I got pretty good at it.

"I just feel like I had a little bit more fun playing football. The game was more fun than baseball or basketball to me. I just enjoy playing it. I felt like when I got to middle school and up in high school, it became more than just a sport I played. It was something I loved to do. That's what really separated it from baseball and basketball. I enjoyed it a little bit more."

His talent was abundant and obvious and would be nurtured to its fullest at Byrnes High School.

If there are high school "football factories," Byrnes certainly qualifies. The school has some of the best facilities in the nation and routinely wins state championships.

With Lattimore at tailback and rushing for 6,375 yards and 108 touchdowns, Byrnes won two state championships and reached the finals Lattimore's senior year.

"Oh, man, it was great," Lattimore said. "I've got a lot of great memories from high school. We were a Nike school and we were on ESPN several times a year. It was something that as a young age we saw it growing up and we knew we wanted to be a part of that. We won a lot of games and a lot of state championships. Everybody there just loves football."

As a senior, Lattimore earned Parade All-American honors, was selected as the state of South Carolina's "Mr. Football" and was rated as either the No. 1 or No. 2 tailback prospect in the nation by the majority of recruiting services.

The recruiting battle for his services narrowed to Auburn and South Carolina.

"With Auburn and South Carolina, both being in the SEC was a really big factor for me," Lattimore said. "Auburn maybe has a little bit better running back tradition than South Carolina, but it came down to my comfort level with the players there. When I went to Auburn, the players were great, but I just didn't feel as comfortable as I did at South Carolina. Just being able to play for a legend like coach [Steve] Spurrier was big too."

THE SETTING

When Lattimore arrived on campus in the summer of 2010, expectations were high at South Carolina that the Gamecocks could be headed for a breakout season.

Several solid recruiting classes led to that optimism, and Lattimore appeared to be a key piece to the puzzle.

That became evident in the second game of the season when he rushed for 182 yards and two touchdowns in the Gamecocks' 17-6 victory over Georgia.

Lattimore continued to run impressively as the season progressed, with the Gamecocks rolling up a record of 6-3.

Marcus Lattimore. *AP Images*

Next on the schedule was a game at Florida, the school where Spurrier won the Heisman Trophy as a player and later coached to the school's first national championship.

A victory over the Gators would clinch South Carolina's first SEC East Championship and send the Gamecocks to Atlanta for the SEC Championhip game.

GAME OF MY LIFE

BY MARCUS LATTIMORE

"The week of practice for the Florida game, it was really intense. We knew coming in that we had a chance to beat them. They were a little bit off that year, but it was still Florida. They had the same athletes. A lot of team speed. And our reputation against Florida wasn't that good. Just leading up to it, we knew the SEC East was on the line and that added extra motivation for us.

"Even being on the road, we were pretty confident going in. Then they returned that first kickoff for a touchdown and it really scared us a little bit. I've never heard a stadium as loud as that stadium. Ever.

"We knew coming in we had to run the ball and manage the clock against them because they had great team speed and a good defense. I wasn't expecting to carry it 40 times but it worked out that way. The inside zone blocking was working and we just stuck with it. If it's working, we're not going to stray from it. That really set us up. [Quarterback Stephen] Garcia also did a great job running the ball and the receivers did a great job blocking downfield and of course the offensive line opened it up for me. Just a great day.

"When we made that first touchdown, I scored on a 7-yard run, and Patrick DiMarco, our fullback, did a great job of taking that defensive end out, and that let me slide in there for the touchdown. We knew right then we could run the ball.

"After that first kickoff and that first drive when we didn't score, they were doing a lot of talking. They were hyped up too. They were at their home stadium, it was a night game, and there was a lot at stake for them too. But the talking stopped after we put up about two more touchdowns and went on to win 36-14.

"It was amazing. I've never experienced anything like it, and neither has South Carolina. We knew we were going to Atlanta to play for the SEC Championship, so everybody was just overjoyed. Coach Spurrier was happy to go back and get a win over the program where he had played and coached. When we got back to Williams-Brice, it seemed like half the stadium was full at 2:30 in the morning. It was an amazing thing to see. It was one of the happiest moments of my life."

THE AFTERMATH

Lattimore finished the Florida game with 212 yards rushing on 40 carries and scored two touchdowns.

The rest of the season proved a bit anticlimactic. South Carolina beat Troy and arch-rival Clemson, but lost to eventual national champion Auburn 56-17 in the SEC Championship game and then lost to Florida State 26-17 in the Chick-fil-A Bowl.

Lattimore played parts of two more seasons for the Gamecocks, with a left knee injury cutting short his sophomore year and a right knee injury ending his junior year.

The second of those two injuries came on Oct. 27, 2012 against Tennessee.

As he lay on the field at Williams-Brice Stadium being attended to by medical personnel, his teammates surrounded him. Just behind them, the entire Tennessee football team gathered in a show of respect.

The injury was severe. Lattimore tore the anterior cruciate, lateral collateral, and posterior cruciate ligaments in his right knee.

The outpouring of support that followed locally, regionally, and nationally made it clear that Lattimore was one of the most respected college athletes in the nation, and certainly one of the most beloved to play for the Gamecocks.

Renowned surgeon Dr. James Andrews performed what was termed a very successful surgery in November.

Lattimore announced soon afterward that he would forego his senior year at South Carolina to turn pro and that he hoped to be ready for the 2013 season.

He finished his college career with 555 carries for 2,677 yards rushing and a school-record 38 rushing touchdowns and a school-record combined 41 touchdowns.

On March 27, 2013, after intensive rehabilitation, he was able to participate on a limited basis in South Carolina's annual Pro Timing Day in front of representatives from all 32 NFL teams.

After watching Lattimore participate in indoor drills, the room burst into applause.

"It was crazy," he said. "I did not expect that at all. Pretty much every scout came up to me and said that it was amazing and inspiring."

The players then moved outdoors for more drills. It was Lattimore's first time back on the playing field at Williams-Brice Stadium since his injury.

"I love Williams-Brice," Lattimore told reporters. "This is where it all started. There are a lot of memories. I love being back. It is a blessing. I'm grateful that I was raised here and was able to play for my home state and it's going to be great 10 years from now coming back."

When he does return, Lattimore says it will be with no regrets.

"When I got there, I never would have imagined everything that happened, the good and the bad," he said. "I wouldn't change one thing that happened because I was just being myself. With all the love I received at Carolina, even from Clemson fans, I was just being myself the whole time. The only way I can really sum my career is just one that I'll never regret. It was the best time of my life."